Introduction To
Movement Education

"A First Step Toward an Understanding and Application of the Concepts, Methods, and Analyses of Movement Education."

Introduction To Movement Education

An
INDIVIDUALIZED
Approach
To Teaching
Physical
Education

Glenn Kirchner
Jean Cunningham
Eileen Warrell

Simon Fraser University

WM. C. BROWN COMPANY PUBLISHERS
Dubuque, Iowa

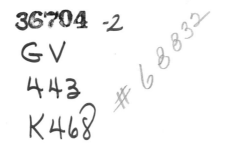

ACKNOWLEDGMENTS

The authors wish to express their gratitude to Mr. George Nelson, Superintendent of School District 43 (Coquitlam, B. C.), to the Physical Education Supervisor, Mr. George Longstaff, to the Principal, Mr. Robert McBay, and to the staff of Porter Street School, for their generous assistance and cooperation. Much of the information contained in this book is the direct result of teaching with a Movement Education approach to the children of this school. To each teacher and pupil our sincere thanks.

We also wish to extend our appreciation to Mr. Harold Kirchner for his contributions to the technical drawings, and to Mr. Al Sens and Mr. Chris Hildred for their advice and technical assistance with the illustrations of this book. Finally, we wish to express our sincere appreciation to our secretary, Mrs. Doris Muzzlewhite, for her resourcefulness at all times.

Dedicated To The Children And Staff Of Porter Street School

PREFACE

Once in a very long time an exciting idea arises in education and captures the interest of our profession. Movement Education is rapidly promising to become a major trend in the elementary school programs of Canada and the United States. New programs are being initiated throughout these countries, major conferences are devoting increased time to this subject, and teacher education programs are now beginning to use the Movement Education approach in the training of future classroom teachers.

This book represents an initial contribution to the understanding of Movement Education. In order to determine how this approach could be introduced into the elementary school physical education programs on this continent, the authors entered into a joint project with a local school district. For a period of one year Jean Cunningham and Eileen Warrell taught with a Movement Education approach the children in Kindergarten through Grade Seven. The normal program in this school prior to our project was typical in its class size, previous physical education experience, and time allotment. The format and content of this book have been strongly influenced by the day to day developments of this project. We have also drawn upon the combined experiences of Jean Cunningham and Eileen Warrell who have used this approach for the past fifteen years with children in England, Jamaica, the United States, and Canada.

Part One provides the basic information concerning purposes, content, and methods of instruction. These introductory chapters provide the necessary background for understanding the two subsequent programs in Parts Two and Three, as well as a working guide for teachers wishing to develop their own Movement Education Programs.

Parts Two and Three contain nine themes which represent a full year's program of Movement Education. Since this approach, in format and teaching techniques, is fundamentally different from much in contemporary physical education, numerous detailed lessons have been included in the primary and intermediate sections. The illustrations that accompany each lesson are not considered to be decorative or "page fillers." On the contrary, each illustration and diagram is intended to give the reader a visual image of what kinds of movement patterns to expect from this approach to teaching physical education.

Part Four is a resource file describing available audiovisual resources, diagrams, and descriptions of commercial and inexpensive equipment. We have also listed the names and addresses of Movement Education experts who are available for workshops and for other consulting services.

It is our sincere hope that Introduction to Movement Education will assist classroom teachers in experimenting with, and hopefully adopting, Movement Education as a basic approach to teaching gymnastics and other forms of physical activity.

CONTENTS

PART ONE

Movement Education in the Physical Education Program

Chapter   Page

1. Physical Education in Contemporary Education 3

   Physical Education in the New Curriculum 4
   The Meaning and Role of Movement Education 4
   The Educational Values of Movement Education 6

2. Curriculum Organization 13

   Structure of a Movement Education Curriculum 13
   Instructional Time for Movement Education 15
   Teaching by Themes 17

3. Methods of Instruction 21

   Methods Used in Movement Education 21
   Structure of a Lesson Plan 25
   Allocation of Time Within Each Lesson 29
   Observation and Progression of Skills 29

PART TWO

A Movement Education Program for Primary Grades

4. Theme One: Safety Training 33

   The Attitude of the Teacher 34
   The Attitude of the Children 38

5. Theme Two: Adding to the Range and Understanding of Movement 66

6. Theme Three: Understanding Direction 93

7. Theme Four: Qualities 118

PART THREE
A Movement Education Program for Intermediate Grades

8. Theme One: Safety Training 139

How to Begin 140

9. Theme Two: Adding to the Range and Understanding of Movement 155

Assessment of Previous Lessons 166

10. Theme Three: Stretching and Curling 167

11. Theme Four: Change of Direction 177

12. Theme Five: Twisting 186

Qualities of Movement 202

PART FOUR
Appendixes

Appendix A. Instructional Aids and Human Resources 207

Visual Aids 207

Human Resources 214

Written Materials 217

Appendix B. Apparatus, Equipment, and Supplies 221

Small Apparatus 221

Large Apparatus 228

Agility or Climbing Apparatus 232

Appendix C. Definition of Terms Used in Movement Education 237

Appendix D. Apparatus, Equipment, and Supply Companies 241

Index 245

PART ONE

Movement Education
in the Physical Education
Program

CHAPTER ONE

Physical Education in Contemporary Education

Physical Education in the New Curriculum

The Meaning and Role of Movement Education

The Educational Values of Movement Education

Education is in a state of turbulence and has been ever since the end of World War II. The great debate about the aims, techniques, and environment of education has spread far outside the ranks of educators. We now live in an age where the television screen, the magazine, and the paperback have brought searing criticism as well as thoughtful appraisal of education directly into the home.

Through such representative titles as "How *Does* John Learn to Read?"— "Lifetimes of Miseducation"—and "How to Damage the Nation's Children," we find a growing realization of the vital importance of the preschool and elementary school years. These early years are without doubt the most formative in the physical, emotional, and intellectual development of the child.

Amid all the criticism and dissent, there are many encouraging ideas, new and progressive ideas, most of which must inevitably take a long time to become established. A few, however, such as the nongraded school and the use of para-professionals in teaching, are more or less accepted now. No discipline and no area of school life should be free from constant questioning, and educators who for too long accepted their traditional role with self-confidence are now beginning to reassess their fundamental aims.

Physical education, along with most subject areas in the elementary school, is undergoing such questioning and reassessment. Movement Education, the subject of this book, is a direct result of critical analysis, fundamental questioning, and practical experimentation.

Physical Education in the New Curriculum

In the process of developing a new elementary school physical education program, consideration must be given to the evidence available from such sources as growth and development, motor learning, and other related fields. There is, for example, adequate evidence that children of the same age are not at the same stage in physiological maturity. Within any grade there may be as much as five years' difference in the physiological maturity of the children. This factor alone has many implications for the kind of physical activities taught. Children need vigorous physical activity daily if they are to develop to their highest physical and mental potential. However, this does not mean all children should take the same exercise and perform at the same rate. It is equally important to consider the initial level of physical fitness of each child and plan his program accordingly.

Not only do children of a given age group reveal wide discrepancies in physical abilities, they also exhibit very different attitudes and reactions in the gymnasium. For instance, one particular child may be an outstanding performer in team games and yet achieve little success in gymnastics or dance. In part this may be a matter of attitudes, but the teacher cannot ignore the possibility that social psychological factors are also at work here. Perhaps this same child—and particularly if he is a boy—will be mentally conditioned to consider team games as legitimate expression of a tough masculinity, whereas dance could be a correspondingly miserable experience because it would seem to detract from the same masculine image. This is not the invariable reaction, and it is interesting to remember that in many warrior societies dancing is specifically a male occupation, but in the cultural background for which this book is intended it is certainly more common to expect sharp personal preferences among the children. If physical education is to make a really valuable contribution to the life of the elementary school then it must be taught with understanding and vitality, using the most flexible teaching techniques in order to include every child as an enthusiastic participant.

The Meaning and Role of Movement Education

Movement Education may be defined as an individualized approach or system of teaching children to become aware of their physical abilities and to use them effectively in their daily activities involving play, work, and creative expression.[1] Through the medium of gymnastics, using small equipment such as hoops, beanbags, ropes, and large equipment such as a vaulting box or climbing apparatus, a child learns basic movement skills which are

---

[1] Marion North, *A Simple Guide to Movement Teaching*, (Exeter: A. Wheaton & Co., 1964), Chapter 1.

appropriate to his physical maturity and general readiness. According to Cameron and Pleasance, two leading authorities in this field, a child develops an understanding not only of what he is doing, but also of how he is doing a particular movement. Hence, by using this approach we are helping each child perform gymnastic movements which involve the whole body in action, in company with the mind, intelligence, and imagination.[2] Movement Education incorporates the natural inclinations of children, such as the desire to move freely, to be creative, and to test their own abilities through a variety of stunts, games, and play apparatus.

The basic aims of Movement Education have been defined by numerous writers, both in England where it originated and in North America where it is now becoming increasingly popular.[3] The writers believe these aims may be stated as follows:

1. To assist children to become physically fit and skillful in a variety of situations. This requires the teacher to help children increase their co-ordination and flexibility of mind as well as body.
2. To teach children to understand movement so they can build movement sequences from their ever-increasing understanding of what, where, and how the body can move.
3. To encourage self-discipline and self-reliance so children can work on their own ideas individually, in pairs, or in a group.
4. To provide maximum enjoyment and opportunities for creative expression.

FIGURE 1.1

[2]W. McD. Cameron and Peggy Pleasance, *Education in Movement*, (Oxford: Basil Blackwell & Mott, Ltd., 1963), Chapter 1.

[3]E. Mauldon and J. Layson, *Teaching Gymnastics*, (London: MacDonald & Evans, Ltd., 1965), p. 12.

FIGURE 1.2

FIGURE 1.3

The Educational Values of Movement Education

If the principles and procedures of Movement Education are effectively utilized in teaching gymnastics and other physical activities, the following values will be experienced.[4]

---

[4]W. McD. Cameron and Peggy Pleasance, *Education In Movement*, (Oxford: Basil Blackwell & Mott, Ltd. 1963).

Values to the Student

1. The muscular and organic systems of the body will be exercised in a natural and functional way. Through the application of this approach a child's physical attributes, such as his strength, endurance, coordination, and flexibility, are developed in a natural and functional manner.

FIGURE 1.4

2. The level of motor skill of each child will be increased according to his ability, readiness, and interest. This approach permits the outstanding performer to progress as rapidly as he is capable of moving, since he is not held back by slower members of the class. Also, the less able students are not measured against an arbitrary standard or norm, so they too can achieve success and personal satisfaction while participating in realistic tasks and challenges.

FIGURE 1.5

3. The social awarness of each child is fostered by the natural and informal setting of the group. A child must learn to work as a member of a group as well as to work individually within the group. In this way he will learn the meaning of tolerance and will develop the qualities of self-reliance, courage, and self-direction.

FIGURE 1.6

4. The possibility of accidents and injury, particularly on apparatus, is greatly reduced. One of the most important features of this approach is the "built-in" safety which is fostered, in fact emphasized, in every aspect of Movement Education. A "movement task" or challenge is first given by the teacher, to which each child is allowed to respond in his own way. To illustrate, a teacher presents a challenge such as "Can you find a balance position using your head and two other parts of your body?" A child who has sufficient arm and shoulder girdle strength may respond by doing a headstand. Equally correct, however, would be a position in which perhaps a

FIGURE 1.7   **FIGURE 1.8**

less able child uses his head, one foot, and a hand to form a three point balance position. This way of teaching provides "built-in" safety, because when children are given the freedom to evolve their own solutions, they will not attempt a movement which is beyond their capabilities.

It must be emphasized that the above statement is not just an opinion held by the writers. Several studies in England, where Movement Education has been taught for over fifteen years, have shown that the incidence of accidents is dramatically lower than in other programs employing more traditional teaching practices. Throughout the nine months of the authors' recent Movement Education project involving children from Kindergarten to Grade Seven, not one accident occurred.

In traditional gymnastics program all children are required to perform the same stunt. Asking a child who is grossly overweight or physically weak to perform a headstand not only invites accidents but also creates poor attitudes on the part of the less able performer. The approach used in Movement Education encompasses the physical and intellectual abilities and limitations of each performer.

Values to the Teacher

From the teacher's point of view, Movement Education has several advantages over the more contemporary methods currently used in teaching physical activities to children. These are:

1. The teacher has an opportunity to learn more about each child's personality in a noncompetitive and self-expressive situation. The underlying principle of Movement Education is that children progress according to their own ability and at their own rate. With the additional opportunity of providing their own answers to each movement task, each child is able to achieve immediate success and satisfaction. The child judges himself; he knows whether his performance is above or below his capability. Many teachers in the Porter Street project commented that they saw the "low achievers" and "problem cases" of the classroom in a quite different perspective in the gymnasium. The removal of competitive pressure and the risk

of failure created a much more positive attitude toward learning. Furthermore, the personal success experienced by these children in the gymnasium built up their confidence and, in turn, they began to do much better in the classroom. Although these are opinions, related research indicates that success achieved in one area may genuinely motivate achievement in another area.

2. Adoption of classroom methods and mannerisms to the gymnasium. One of the most distinguishing features of Movement Education is the use by the teacher of a natural conversational speaking voice instead of formal commands and the eliminaiton of the whistle as a means of gaining attention and control. In addition, teachers are not required to wear a gymnastic uniform since few demonstrations need to be given by the teacher. This, therefore, eliminates the need for the teacher to be a highly skilled performer; she still may be an effective teacher of Movement Education. Initially, the classroom teacher employs the same methods and techniques used in the classroom to the gymnasium. Gradually, as she acquires an understanding of movement and its analysis, she can refine her approach and use those methods and techniques which prove to be successful for her in teaching Movement Education.

A note of caution. It would be unfair to the physical education profession to infer that teachers no longer need to be skilled in a variety of physical activities, or to infer that they should never demonstrate. It would be equally wrong to imply that they can teach effectively without any theoretical background. This background, however, can be considerably developed by reading, viewing films, active participation in physical education workshops, and observing specialist teachers.

Movement Education is, therefore, one integral part of the physical education program, not its replacement. It is a unique approach to the learning process, and we believe it is complimentary to the total elementary school physical education program.

3. The teacher becomes a "guider" rather than a "director" of the learning experience of each child. Perhaps the most significant change involved in the Movement Education approach is the role of the teacher. She must stimulate her class by providing suitable tasks, but the onus is on the children to solve the problem. While their own ideas and solutions are valuable, equally important are the effects of seeing and trying other children's solutions to the same task. The teacher will often select the most appropriate ideas to extend and challenge the whole class. After this initial period of exploration by the children, and selection by the teacher, (more experienced children may select as well), comes the stage of linking two or three or more movements together to form a sequence or "movement sentence." Repeated practice of these sequences is now essential to improve the quality and standard of performance and provide a sense of achievement. Thus we have four separate stages:

Exploration   *Selection*   *Repetition*   *Polish*

4. The teacher has time for individualized instruction. Since there are no formal lines or commands which require all of the children to perform the same movements at the same time, the teacher continuously circulates among the children. There is no front or back of a class. From any position in the gymnasium the teacher may present a movement problem. Once the problem is understood, all children are actively engaged in its solution in accordance with their own physical abilities and imaginations. While the children are working on their movement ideas, the teacher moves about giving additional suggestions or individual attention wherever she or a child feels assistance is necessary.

FIGURE 1.10

Most teachers will find the transition to this informal setting difficult, particularly during the early stages when children are learning to work on their own. Gradually, however, a teacher will find she can eliminate structured formations and replace the whistle with the natural conversational tone of her own voice. The end result of this transition is an informal atmosphere in which the teacher becomes a guider of the learning experience, applying many methods and techniques according to the needs and interests of the children.

The essential purpose of this book is to provide the teacher who is making a start in this new approach with lesson plans and a lot of practical advice.[5] Needless to say, we appreciate and sympathize with those making this transition from the "formal" to the "informal" approach for the first time. We have, therefore, attempted to lead the beginning teacher toward the "guiding role" as gently as possible. Initial emphasis is on direct teaching allowing informal and scattered formations. Gradually the limitation and indirect methods are introduced until an informal atmosphere is created with the teacher acting as the guider of the learning experience of each child.

---

[5]For films on Movement Education produced by the authors of this book, see Appendix.

REFERENCES

1. BRUNER, JEROME S., *Towards a Theory of Instruction,* Cambridge, Mass.: The Belknap Press of Harvard Press, 1966.
2. CAMERON, W. McD., and PLEASANCE, PEGGY, *Education in Movement,* Oxford: Basil Blackwell & Mott, Ltd., 1965.
3. CRATTY, BRYANT J., *Movement Behavior and Motor Learning,* 2nd Edition, Philadelphia: Lea and Febiger, 1967.
4. CRATTY, BRYANT J., and SISTER MARGARET MARY MARTIN, *Perceptual-Motor Efficiency in Children,* Philadelphia: Lea and Febiger, 1969.
5. HALSEY, ELIZABETH, *Inquiry and Invention in Physical Education,* Philadelphia: Lea and Febiger, 1964.
6. KIRCHNER, G., *Physical Education for Elementary School Children,* Second Edition, Dubuque: Wm. C. Brown Company Publishers, 1970.
7. MAULDIN, E., and LAYSON, J., *Teaching Gymnastics*,* London: MacDonald & Evans, Ltd., 1965.
8. NORTH, MARION, *A Simple Guide to Movement Teaching*,* Exeter: A. Wheaton & Co., 1964.
9. President's Council on Youth Fitness, *Youth Physical Fitness: Suggested Elements of a School Centered Program,* Washington D. C.: U. S. Government Printing Office, 1961.

SUGGESTED READINGS

Articles

HOWARD, S., "The Movement Education Approach to Teaching in English Elementary Schools," *American Journal for Health, Physical Education, and Recreation,* January, 1967, p. 31.
LOCKS, L. F., "The Movement Movement," *Journal of Health, Physical Education Recreation,* January 1966, p. 26.
LUDWIG, E. A., "Towards an Understanding of Basic Movement Education in the Elementary Schools," *Journal for Health, Physical Education Recreation,* March 1968, p. 27.
SIMONS, W. M. M., "Educational Gymnastics—Its Meaning, Uses and Abuses," *Canadian Journal of Health, Physical Education, and Recreation,* p. 6.
WISEMAN, E. D., "Movement Education—What it is and What it is not," *Canadian Journal of Health, Physical Education, and Recreation,* p. 6.

Books

HALSEY, ELIZABETH AND PORTER, LORENA, *Physical Education for Children,* 2nd Edition, New York: Holt, Rinehart & Winston, Inc., 1967.
Inner London Education Authority, *Educational Gymnastics*,* London: 1966.
LABAN, R., AND ULLMANN, L., *The Mastery of Movement*,* London: MacDonald & Evans, Ltd., 1960.
LABAN, R., *Modern Educational Dance*,* London: MacDonald & Evans, Ltd., 1948, Ontario Department of Education, *Physical Education Health, Interim Revision* Toronto: 1967.
Ministry of Education, *Moving and Growing,* London: Her Majesty's Stationery Office*, 1952.
Ministry of Education, *Planning the Program*,* London: Her Majesty's Stationery Office, 1965.

*All books listed with an asterisk may be purchased from the Ling Book Shop, Ling House, 10 Nottingham Place, London. W. C. 1.

TWO

Curriculum Organization

Structure of a Movement Education Curriculum
Instructional Time for Movement Education
Teaching by Themes

One of the main tasks within the instructional program is to choose the activities and methods that will most effectively realize the objectives of physical education. This, of course, is no mean task since the teacher must be able to distinguish among the various types of physical activities, know where to place the greatest emphasis, and be able to plan a program in a logical and sequential pattern. The content of contemporary physical education programs is usually divided into these broad activity areas: games, dance, and gymnastic or self-testing activities. A teacher selects the kinds of activities she wishes to teach throughout the year and plans her program according to the needs and ages of the children, available facilities and equipment, and the time allotment for physical education.

Each of the activity areas are usually organized into "units" of instruction and taught on the basis of a systematic progression from the simple to the more complex skills. Movement Education is differently arranged in content and in teaching. In the remainder of this chapter the format and structure of a Movement Education program will be clarified for the reader. This chapter will, therefore, provide the teacher with a basis for evaluating the two suggested programs presented in Parts Two and Three and will present basic guides for developing her own program.

Structure of a Movement Education Curriculum

There is a fundamental distinction that must be made between the organizational structure of contemporary Physical Education and Movement

Education. In the former, *the activity itself* (volleyball, track and field or folk dance) provides *the structural basis* for developing a curriculum. Skills within each area are arranged from the simple to the complex and presented to children in accordance with their physical maturity and general readiness.

Within the organizational structure of Movement Education, the concepts and underlying principles of "body awareness," "space," and "qualities" of movement provide a basis for *understanding* all movement. In Movement Education, *all* activities are selected on the basis of how well they can foster and develop the concepts and movement principles described under *body awareness, space,* and *qualities* of movement. These concepts or *elements of movement* thus become the *framework* of a *Movement Education Curriculum*. Each of these important elements are defined in the accompanying paragraphs.

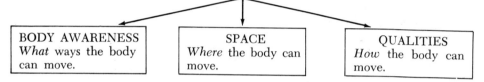

CLASSIFICATION AND BASIS FOR
ANALYZING ALL PHYSICAL MOVEMENT

BODY AWARENESS	SPACE	QUALITIES
What ways the body can move.	*Where* the body can move.	*How* the body can move.

Body Awareness—What Ways the Body Can Move

Body awareness is the recognition of the way in which the body or parts of it can be controlled, moved, and balanced upon. This category includes the four basic actions of *stretching, bending, twisting,* and *turning*.

Space—Where the Body Can Move

FIGURE 2.1   FIGURE 2.2

Space, the second related aspect of movement, refers to the amount of space a movement requires and the direction of the movement.

All the space a child can reach out to from a fixed position, such as from standing on the floor or from sitting on a bench, is known as his *personal space*. When a child moves away from a fixed base he is moving through *general space*.[1]

Within these two special aspects of "personal" and "general" space a child learns to move in a forward, backward, sideways, and a diagonal direction. He also learns to travel at high, medium, and low levels on the floor, in relation to himself, a partner, or in relation to each piece of apparatus.

Qualities—How the Body Can Move

FIGURE 2.3

Qualities, the third element of movement, describes the ability to move the body quickly or slowly, to perform light or strong movements, and the ability to link one movement to another with control and efficiency.[2]

Instructional Time for Movement Education

Since the majority of classroom teachers are responsible for their own physical education programs, the amount of time devoted to Movement Education will, in essence, depend upon whether or not the teacher is convinced of the values inherent in this approach to teaching physical education. Therefore, the following time allotments are only suggested guidelines.

---

[1]W. McD. Cameron and Peggy Pleasance, *Education in Movement,* (Oxford: Basil Blackwell & Mott, Ltd., 1965), p. 7.

[2]Inner London Education Authority, *Movement Education for Infants,* London, 1966, p. 11.

In the Primary Grades

In a previous section, it was stated that the contemporary physical education program consisted of the three broad areas of games, dance, and gymnastic or self-testing activities.[3] If primary teachers organize their yearly program along contemporary lines, they usually allocate approximately one-third of the total year's program to each respective area. This is illustrated in the accompanying pie diagram.

Although it is possible to include all the games, dance, and gymnastic skills in a primary Movement Education program, the writers do not recommend this to be done by those teachers who are beginning to use the Movement Education approach for the first time. It is wise to begin to teach Movement Education through the medium of gymnastics self-testing activities until not only a "movement vocabulary" has been created, but there is an understanding of elements of movements and theme construction, and a clear idea of how to analyze and correct movement skills and ideas has been developed by the teacher. It may take anywhere from several months to a year before she feels qualified to extend the Movement Education approach into the games and dance areas. As a general guideline, devote approximately one-third of your initial program to Movement Education in the gymnastic area. Plan the remaining two-thirds of your program to game skills and appropriate dance activities. Whenever you feel capable, begin to experiment with the Movement Education approach within the dance and games areas. Eventually, it is possible for primary teachers to include all the basic skills of games, dance, and gymnastics within a comprehensive Movement Education Program.

---

[3]G. Kirchner, *Physical Education for Elementary School Children*, Second Edition, (Dubuque: Wm. C. Brown Company Publishers, 1970).

In the Intermediate Grades

The application of Movement Education to virtually all activities in the intermediate grades becomes more difficult. As indicated in Chapter 1, a child who has been exposed to four or five years of a teacher-directed program and is then suddenly given a new format for learning may feel somewhat insecure and resistant to this new approach. At the same time, skills, rules, and team play in the games of volleyball, basketball, and softball, may be more effectively taught by contemporary methods rather than by the Movement Education approach, although *understanding* movement is bound to assist the teaching and learning of any game.

In the accompanying diagram, Movement Education is recommended as the basic instructional approach to all gymnastic type activities. Depending on the student's background in dance as well as the teacher's own ability, Movement Education may be used to lead into the teaching of creative dance.

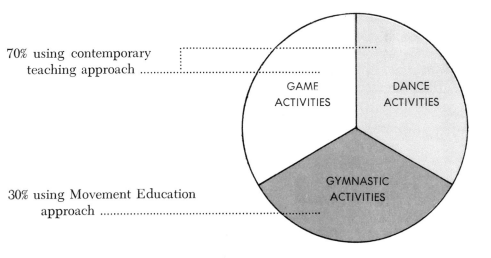

70% using contemporary teaching approach

GAME ACTIVITIES

DANCE ACTIVITIES

GYMNASTIC ACTIVITIES

30% using Movement Education approach

Teaching by Themes

The most common teaching pattern currently used in the elementary school is the "instructional unit." In the physical education program, a unit of volleyball may be taught for a period of time ranging from two to six weeks. Within the unit, skills, rules, and lead-up games are organized and presented in a systematic fashion, but no other activities from the gymnastic or dance areas are usually taught while the unit is being "covered."

It is impossible to have a Movement Education program this way as there must be continuity from one part of the program to the next throughout the year and in each succeeding year. As stressed in the previous section, this approach need not interfere with the instructional unit approach to teaching games or dance activities, providing there is at least one gymnastics lesson each week with a Movement Education approach as the link or core of the program.

Our discussion of themes will now be restricted to those activities which would normally be tackled in the gymnasium, with or without apparatus. Intermediate teachers who wish to explore the use of movement education to teaching game and dance skills can effectively use the examples provided in the gymnastic area as a basic guideline.

How a Theme Is Developed

A theme may be defined as a central movement idea that is to be emphasized in a series of lessons.

In the theme of "flight" we wish to explore all the ways the body can be propelled into the air, the shapes or positions it can make in the air, and the ways in which the weight of the body can be recovered on landing.

FIGURE 2.4   **FIGURE 2.5**

In the course of the theme and at the appropriate part of the lesson the children would practice such movements as:

FIGURE 2.6

1. Jumping and leaping freely, or over small apparatus such as hoops or ropes.
2. Dropping from a height such as the vaulting box, the stage, or the wall bars, on to a mat where the emphasis is on a controlled landing which leads directly into a forward or tucked roll, (see "Safety Training," Chapter 4).
3. Jumping into the air to show a specific shape, such as "wide," "narrow," or "twisted," and landing on the feet again.

4. Taking weight directly on the arms, as in cat-springs or crouch vaults, and
5. Leaping onto and swinging on ropes, hanging, and jumping off.

The lesson plans should clarify the importance of relating the movement theme to each piece of apparatus and from lesson to lesson. Instead of concentrating on a few lessons on specific vaulting movements, as is done in traditional gymnastics, movements involving "flight" are explored in a number of ways on the floor and on a variety of challenging apparatus in each lesson and continuously throughout the theme. Subsidiary themes may be introduced and a wide variety of activities will be performed during *each* lesson.

One could think of a theme in the following way. Imagine someone who has always eaten potatoes for one week, dessert for two weeks, vegetable for a week, and meat for three weeks. His digestion works perfectly well and he feels comfortable with this form and type of nourishment. We are now inviting this person to experiment with what might seem to be a bizarre arrangement, by asking him to have a little meat, potato, and vegetable followed by a little dessert at each meal. At this stage he must take our word for it that he will not get violent indigestion. After getting used to it, he will feel fitter and even enjoy it.

The second important point about teaching by themes is that it provides tremendous opportunities for individual interpretation. To illustrate, during a theme of "stretch and curl," the teacher may have asked the children, after some preliminary work, to choose two stretch and two curl positions and link them into a continuous movement pattern. "Begin by going from your first stretch position into your first curl position."

Child "A" might have produced the following response. Her "stretch" was performed while lying on the floor face down with toes and fingertips all involved with the stretch and she may have followed this with a roll on to her side and into a tight tucked curl. (Figure 2.7)

Child "B," on the other hand, may perform a handstand to represent the "stretch" position, then bend her elbows, tuck her head under, and move straight into a forward roll for her "curled" position. (Figure 2.8)

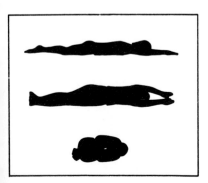

FIGURE 2.7

FIGURE 2.8

Both children have responded according to their natural abilities and interests. Both had to think out a solution in relation to the theme. Both are correct.

Although we may have convinced some readers of the desirability of teaching Movement Education, there must still be many unanswered questions and a degree of apprehension in attempting to teach by this approach. Since this is a "first" stage, the writers have provided detailed lesson plans to start with, gradually shifting to note-form suggestions. Each of these lessons has been successfully taught to children who were used to a traditional approach.

In the initial stages of teaching by themes, most teachers will find themselves moving from one theme to the next, taking between three to six lessons per theme. As the teacher and children become experienced, more time will be spent on each theme. This is due to the fact that as the children's movement vocabulary increases, the teacher will be able to expand and utilize the children's ideas.

Teaching by theme not only harnesses the exploratory approach but also gives it a *purpose* and a *challenge,* thus making it a highly effective teaching method. Further, movement skills and ideas learned in one theme carry over to each succeeding theme, thus constantly expanding and enriching the movement skills and understanding of each child.

REFERENCES

1. KIRCHNER, G., *Physical Education for Elementary School Children,* Second Edition, Dubuque: Wm. C. Brown Company Publishers, 1970.
2. MAULDON E. and LAYSON, J., *Teaching Gymnastics,* London: MacDonald & Evans, Ltd., 1965.

SUGGESTED READINGS

BILBROUGH, A., AND JONES, P., *Physical Education in the Primary Schools,* London: University of London Press, Ltd., 1965.

BOGER, M. H., *The Teaching of Elementary School Physical Education,* New York: J. Lowell Pratt & Co., 1965.

CAMERON, W. McD., AND PLEASANCE, PEGGY, *Education in Movement,* Oxford: Basil Blackwell & Mott, Ltd., 1965.

HALSEY, E., AND PORTER, L., *Physical Education for Children,* 2nd Edition, New York: Holt, Rinehart & Winston, Inc., 1967.

Ministry of Education, *Planning the Program,* London: Her Majesty's Stationery Office, 1965.

MOSTON, M., *Developmental Movement,* Columbus: Charles E. Merrill Publishing Co., 1965.

NORTH, M., *A Simple Guide to Movement Teaching,* Exeter: A. Wheaton & Co., 1964.

RANDALL, M., *Basic Movement,* London: Bell & Sons, Ltd., 1963.

CHAPTER THREE

Methods of Instruction

Methods Used in Movement Education
Structure of a Lesson Plan
Allocation of Time Within Each Lesson
Observation and Progression of Skills

Methods Used in Movement Education

A method or technique is selected on the basis of its contribution to the aims of the program. Equally important is its appropriateness to the basic principles of learning, the personality of the teacher, and the unique characteristics of the children.

Numerous authors have attempted to define Movement Education simply and aptly. Since it has so many facets and possesses such a large ingredient of "personal interpretation," simple definitions are difficult to state.[1]

The writers believe it is not just a unique content area of physical education, nor is it a unique form of organizing movement experiences or just one specific method of teaching. It is all these factors blended together which clearly characterize it as a distinctive approach to learning through the medium of physical activity.

A great deal is known about how children learn and what the optimum conditions for learning are.[2] We know that children learn best when they are "involved," interested, and genuinely eager to know.[3] We also know that

---

[1]E. Mauldon and J. Layson, *Teaching Gymnastics,* (London: MacDonald & Evans, Ltd., 1965). Chapter 1.

[2]C. E. Davis & E. C. Wallis, *Towards Better Teaching in Physical Education,* (Englewood Cliffs: Prentice-Hall, Inc., 1961). Chapter 11.

[3]J. R. Braun, *Contemporary Research in Learning,* (New York: D. Van Nostrand Co., Inc., 1963).

children may be stimulated and "involved" by the teacher in a variety of ways. A method that is good for Mr. X may not work with Miss Y. Another approach may be very effective for both Mr. X and Miss Y for nine classes out of ten. The tenth class may be different. On Monday Mr. X might feel like patiently drawing some piece of information out of the class. On Tuesday, he may simply "tell" them, in order to move quickly on to something else.

No experienced teacher would ever agree that there is one method superior to all the others. In Movement Education all the known and time honored methods are used, and not just the exploratory or indirect method.

We have implied that your teaching method or "your approach" will not depend solely on how you are feeling or how your class is responding to you. The methods you employ with any class at any time will be a direct reflection of the total learning situation.[4]

Clearly, then, the aims of Movement Education and our knowledge of the learning process indicate there is no single method that can meet all of our needs. Each teacher must draw upon a variety of appropriate methods according to her own ability and use them on the basis of helping each child to develop new insights and movement skills. The most popular methods currently used in Movement Education are described in the next section. They are direct, indirect, and limitation methods of instruction. As a general guideline, teachers should use all three methods. The direct method may be used during the early stages of introducing Movement Education and then gradually increase the use of the indirect and limitation methods. The reasons underlying this basic suggestion are given under each description.

Direct Method

In the direct method of instruction the teacher structures the classroom organizational pattern, chooses the type of activity, and prescribes what and how each child in the class should execute the movement skill or ideas involved. Example—Learning the forward roll.

FIGURE 3.1

[4]N. Cantor and S. M. Corey, *The Teaching-Learning Process,* (New York: Holt, Rinehart & Winston, Inc., 1953), Chapter 12.

1. Class Organization. In a traditional gymnastic lesson, children are usually arranged in a line formation on the long side of the mat. In Movement Education there are no lines or line-ups and this is where individual mats are invaluable to the beginning teacher, as each child has his own "spot" and yet the class has free spacing.
2. Choice of Activity. Let us imagine a lesson where forward rolls are being performed. Many people appear to be banging their heads instead of tucking them under. The teacher would stop the whole class, give the relevant coaching points, and invite everyone to try again, keeping in mind what has just been said.

The latter case is an example of the direct method since all children are required to perform the same activity.

Although this method of instruction has many shortcomings with respect to developing initiative and self-direction, it may be used when the following is desired: (1) To teach a specific movement skill, safety procedure, or a rule correctly and effectively, and (2) To allow the whole class to practice a specific skill or movement idea which the teacher feels should have general attention and improvement.

Indirect Method

In the indirect method of instruction the children are given the opportunity to choose the activity or movement idea to be practiced. They also have the freedom to use any piece of apparatus that is available in the gymnasium.

The distinguishing feature of this method is the freedom or opportunity given to each child to practice on the floor or on any apparatus that is available. In the illustration given below, the mats, springboard, benches, and hoops are scattered throughout the gymnasium. Since the "instruction" is "practice freely on any movement idea," each child has the freedom to use the floor or any piece of equipment that interests him.

FIGURE 3.2

The Indirect Method: (1) Recognizes individual differences in abilities and interests. (2) Allows the teacher to determine what children like to perform. (3) Encourages initiative and self-direction.

Limitation Method

The limitation method is actually a compromise between the direct method and indirect method. In this case, the choice of an activity or movement is limited *in some way* by the teacher.

FIGURE 3.3

Example: "Travel from one end of the bench to the other,
keeping one foot in contact with it."

The limitation method appears to be used most frequently since it allows skills to be learned in an informal setting with the teacher placing limitations and emphasis according to the needs of the children. The following advantages seem to support the general adoption of this method of instruction:

1. It allows for some direction to be given by the teacher, yet the "free" or creative expressions of children are not hampered.
2. It allows for individual differences in physical ability and personal interest of each child.
3. The analysis and correction of movements by the teacher is simplified because one type of movement is to be practiced by all children, thus general teaching points can be identified.

The three methods of instruction should not be considered as separate entities even within the framework of a single lesson. In Movement Education, a teacher will use a combination of all three, the emphasis dependent upon what and how a particular movement skill or idea is to be learned.

Structure of a Lesson Plan

It is important to recognize that in Movement Education the need for a lesson plan or what might be better defined as a "flexible framework" is very important in the day-to-day development of a theme. Hence, the basic structure of a typical lesson will be outlined beforehand, and the approximate proportion of time that should be spent in each area will have been determined.

In gymnastics a Movement Education lesson consists of an *Introductory Activity* followed by one section of *Movement Training* and one of *Apparatus Work*. The essential aspects of each section will be discussed under the appropriate headings.

TYPICAL LESSON PLAN

Free Practice Before Lesson Begins
Part 1: INTRODUCTORY ACTIVITY —general practice
Part II: MOVEMENT TRAINING —floor work without apparatu.
Part III: APPARATUS WORK —use of small and large apparatus

"Bonus" or Free Practice Before Lesson Begins

One of the most striking characteristics of a Movement Education lesson is the immediate participation of children as soon as they enter the gymnasium. Since every teaching situation varies with respect to where and how long it takes children to change and enter the gymnasium, a simple procedure is established to cover this situation: as soon as each child has changed his clothes and is in the gymnasium, he is allowed to practice any previously learned movement pattern or to experiment with small equipment such as balls, beanbags, or hoops. During this time the teacher has an opportunity to supervise the changing, talk to the children, or provide assistance and encouragement wherever she finds it necessary.

The following suggestions may be helpful to teachers in the planning and general supervision of this phase of the lesson:
1. The length of the free practice will vary from class to class depending upon the ages of children and the changing conditions. As a general rule the length of this part of the lesson should be approximately three to four minutes.

FIGURE 3.4

2. Restrict practice to individual movement skill with or without a partner. Do not allow practice in groups or on large apparatus.
3. Have all equipment, such as balls, beanbags, hoops, and small mats, arranged in the gymnasium prior to the arrival of the children in the gymnasium.
4. Do not, however, allow for any horseplay during this period. It should be a period of constructive practice.
5. Create a few clear-cut rules regarding changing and entering the gymnasium and insist that all the children abide by them. When procedures are well established the teacher can spend her time in the gymnasium observing and providing individual assistance.

Part I: The Introductory Activity

This first part of the lesson, which should last about five minutes, is related to the "warm-up" of a traditionally planned lesson. Both should be simple to understand so that the children can get started quickly and energetically. Both have the same physiological motives, that of increasing

FIGURE 3.5

the circulation and providing a much needed burst of activity after prolonged sitting. The differences, however, between a "warm-up" and an introductory activity are threefold.
1. The theme of the lesson should be represented. (This will become apparent when the reader starts to use the lesson plans.)
2. Small apparatus such as hoops, beanbags, or balls (benches are very useful here if there are enough) are frequently used.
3. The introductory activity, although simple and energetic, should not be devoid of skill or thoughfulness. It is as important to "coach," stimulate, and "refine" the performance of this part of the lesson as the other two parts.

Part II: Movement Training

This part of the lesson is concerned with the development of movement patterns or sequences which may be designed by the class as a whole, as a result of working with a partner or individually. (See Appendix A for description of Simon Fraser University film 4 entitled "How to Develop a Theme.")

FIGURE 3.6

How to gradually bring the children to the point where they can make up quite lengthy individual sequences will become clear as the teacher follows the lesson plans in Parts Two and Three. Some rules to bear in mind, however, when planning this part of the lesson are:
1. Teach the children one aspect of your theme and let them explore possible variations, or at least give them a problem that is clearly explained and within their capabilities. DO NOT give them a vague request in broad terms such as "Do any movement sequence which shows a variation of speed." The latter may be appropriate for an experienced class, but would leave a beginning class floundering.

2. Exploration will come about as a result of these suggestions: "Can you do it another way?" or "Do the same thing from a different starting position."
3. Would the movement idea benefit by combining with a partner or a group?
4. After a movement problem has been presented to the class, allow sufficient time for the children to think about it and work out their ideas. A teacher should always have some ideas of her own so that she can give an example of one way of tackling the problem, if necessary.

This part of the lesson should last about ten minutes, after which time they should gather into their groups (six in each) for the apparatus work.

Part III: Apparatus Work

It is often said of this part of the lesson that the movement ideas explored on the floor in movement training are then applied to the apparatus. This is generally true. However, there are exceptions which will be discussed in Parts Two and Three. The large apparatus such as benches, box stage, and springboard, present a new set of challenges in terms of height from the ground, shape, and general design.

During the movement training part of the lesson the basic movement ideas of the themes are explored. Following this, children should attempt to apply the ideas they developed on the floor to the new media of apparatus. The latter should provide an exciting and stimulating "variation" of the theme. This is not to infer that the same movement sequences performed on the floor are then applied in an identical way to the apparatus. It is the movement ideas that are applied to the apparatus.

After children become accustomed to working independently on the apparatus, the teacher may be able to give them even greater responsibility by saying, "Arrange the benches any way you like in this group" or "Mary, you have a mat and springboard, use any piece of small apparatus and build it into your group's work."

Once children become accustomed to working in this way they will often alter the arrangement of their apparatus if they have thought up an idea which

FIGURE 3.7

calls for change. Change for the sake of changing is obviously a danger and should be discouraged.

Although children within each group use the same apparatus to develop their theme, each child applies his own movement solutions according to his physical abilities and personal creativity.

The following suggestions will be helpful in arranging apparatus and assisting children in expanding their movement ideas on the apparatus.

1. During the first few lessons allow children to freely explore the arrangement and possible use of apparatus or give simple tasks such as "Use all sides of your apparatus" or "go over it one way and under it another way."
2. Teach children of every grade to lift, carry, and arrange their own apparatus. This is not poor or lazy teaching; children must be taught this responsibility.
3. When using more than one piece of apparatus (example: balance beam, climbing ropes, and vaulting box) rotate groups to ensure that all children have an opportunity to practice on each type of apparatus.

Allocation of Time Within Each Lesson

Since the length of physical education periods vary from fifteen minutes to one hour, recommendations with respect to allocating time to Parts I, II, and III must be done on a basis of percentages. Although each part of the lesson is considered of equal importance, the rate of learning a particular movement theme or idea determines the amount of time to be respectively allocated. Hence, when a movement education theme is first introduced, allow proportionally more time for the Introductory Activity and for Movement Training and less time for Apparatus work. As the theme develops, allow more time for Apparatus work. Numerous modifications will, of course, be worked out by each teacher. Additional suggestions are provided throughout Parts Two and Three.

Observation and Progression of Skills

Progress is defined as "to develop to a higher, better, and more advanced stage." In Movement Education, a teacher obviously wants each child to develop a deeper understanding of movement and to improve in physical skill. Yet in this approach a child is encouraged to create his own "movement answers" to each movement task. Progress, therefore, is an individual matter and can be judged or evaluated only on this basis. Nevertheless, the teacher must observe and evaluate each child's progress on the basis of some criteria, however subjective and personal it may be. In the initial stages, teachers have difficulty in seeing everyone doing different things and at the same time. We suggest you follow one child for a time, then shift your observation to another in a different part of the room. Gradually you will learn to observe in a different way because you will no longer be observing for uniformity of shape, pattern, and timing. What you learn to observe are different solutions to the same task. It is not possible to see exactly what every child is doing the whole time but then no teacher is ever expected to see exactly what each child is doing when writing a story.

Once the teacher has "found her feet" and can use the indirect and limitation methods of instruction with confidence, she will find that not only she but also the children in her class will become critical observers. This will certainly be the case if she guides the class's thinking and attitudes from the start with the use of individual and group illustrations. These should always be chosen from as wide a range as possible. The teacher should never invite a class to watch Mary because "she is doing it nicely." She should point out that Mary is doing it well because of a, b, and c. Where the indirect and limitation methods have been used and children have developed a wide variety of ideas, the teacher must always say *why* she likes the illustrations she has chosen. This, of course, is the natural tendency of any good teacher, whatever the subject. Due to the practical nature of Movement Education there is an opportunity to encourage each child's appreciation of another's efforts. The teacher of Movement Education encourages *tolerance* of others, and at the same time, awakens the critical and analytical powers of the children. Her own deeper understanding of movement will grow imperceptibly, and by the end of six to eight months, she will have no difficulty in "evaluating" the children's progress.

REFERENCES

1. BILBOUGH, A. AND JONES, P., *Physical Education in the Primary Schools*, London: University of London Press, Ltd., 1965.
2. BRAUN, J. P., *Contemporary Research in Learning*, New York: D. Van Nostrand Co., Inc., 1963.
3. CANTOR, N. AND COREY, S. M., *The Teaching-Learning Process*, New York: Holt, Rinehart & Winston, Inc., 1953.
4. DAVIS, C. E., AND WALLIS, E. L., *Towards Better Teaching in Physical Education*, Englewood Cliffs: Prentice-Hall, Inc., 1961.
5. INNER LONDON EDUCATION AUTHORITY, *Movement Education for Infants*, London: 1966.
6. MAULDON, E., AND LAYSON, J., *Teaching Gymnastics*, London: MacDonald & Evans, Ltd., 1965.

SUGGESTED READINGS

CAMERON, W. McD. AND PLEASANCE, P., *Education in Movement*, Oxford: Basil Blackwell & Mott, Ltd., 1965.
LEMEN, M., "Implications of the Problem Solving Method for Physical Educators," *Journal of Health, Physical Education Recreation*, March, 1966, p. 28.
Ministry of Education, *Planning the Program*, London: Her Majesty's Stationery Office, 1953.
NORTH, M., *A Simple Guide to Movement Teaching*, Fourth Edition, Exeter: A. Wheaton & Co., 1964.
RANDALL, M., *Basic Movement*, London: G. Bell & Sons, Ltd., 1963.

PART TWO

A Movement Education
Program
for Primary Grades

Chapter 4. Theme One: Safety Training
Chapter 5. Theme Two: Adding to the Range and Understanding of Movement
Chapter 6. Theme Three: Understanding Direction
Chapter 7. Theme Four: Qualities

Part Two represents a year's program for Kindergarten through Grade Three. Since the majority of teachers using this book will be embarking upon their first attempt to use the Movement Education approach, numerous lesson plans have been described in detail. Any lesson included within each of the four suggested themes may be, with slight variations, taught to any class in the primary grades. The rationale underlying this statement is logical and valid. In this approach to teaching physical education, children of various ages may be given the same task and layout of apparatus. However, since each child is allowed to respond to each movement task according to his own level of physical ability and creative imagination, sufficient scope and challenge is inherent in any lesson. Further, progression of skill and movement ideas becomes an individualized matter, hence no arbitrary standard of performance can be demanded according to grade level or any other normative standard.

The first two or three lessons of each theme are described and illustrated in some detail. Each succeeding lesson is much briefer, simply because one builds upon each preceding lesson.

Within each theme there are "Lesson Reminders." Once a teacher becomes reasonably familiar with a lesson, she need only refer to the "lesson reminder" as a "quick" reference to movement tasks and general layout of apparatus.

Since Movement Education may be simultaneously introduced to the intermediate grades, Part III is arranged in the same format as that for primary grades. Primary teacher should review Part III to understand the similarities in approach and the differences in the performance of older children.

CHAPTER FOUR

Theme One:
Safety Training

Before a teacher embarks upon her first theme entitled "Safety Training," it is imperative that she fully understand the meaning of this term. In its broadest interpretation, it includes not only the attitudes of the teacher and children toward their work in the gymnasium but an understanding of how to protect oneself on or off apparatus. "Safety training," therefore, is an integral part of any lesson in Movement Education.

FIGURE 4.1   **FIGURE 4.2**

The Attitude of the Teacher

What should be the attitude of the teacher toward the use of the time spent in the gymnasium? Should she regard the gymnasium as an extension of the classroom where thoughtful learning takes place through careful guidance? Is it a place where the teacher motivates the child by finding out for himself, by building his confidence and by interests, by stimulating his imagination? Is it a place where she provides opportunities for responsible and considerate behavior? Perhaps she feels that learning in the classroom is such a strain on the children that their time in the gymnasium must provide a release in the form of noisy and uncontrolled activities. If the latter is the teacher's aim in the gymnasium she should not embark upon a program of Movement Education since its goals are totally incompatible with this point of view.

FIGURE 4.3

Any teacher who does not capitalize on the time spent in the gymnasium to extend and often initiate the learning process is losing a most valuable opportunity. Those who teach physical education have one of the easiest tasks in making learning both interesting and enjoyable. Yet it has often been stated that not all children enjoy physical activity. It is the writers' contention as well as that of many leading experts that it is not the activity which children learn to dislike, it is the way it is taught that creates negative attitudes. When one observes Kindergarten children, particularly at the beginning of the year, one is left with no doubt that the desire for movement is a wonderful and natural phenomenon. However, this phase needs proper guidance and direction as children grow. In most instances, when children

are given unsuitable activities or forced into competitive activities before
they are ready, or made to stand still in a long line before they can have
a turn, then the foundations are laid for negative attitudes toward physical
activity, which may last a lifetime.

FIGURE 4.4

Learning and learning theories do not suddenly stop outside the gymnasium doors; children can learn wherever they are. Few teachers would
think of using a whistle to control children in the classroom or tolerate a
noise level where only a whistle could restore order. Why then is it often
thought essential in the gymnasium? (Apart from sports such as volleyball
and basketball, etc., where the whistle is used for officiating.) The range
of the human voice can much more effectively express approval or disapproval.
One simply cannot build confidence or stimulate imagination with a whistle.

In addition to the attitude of the teacher, already discussed, what can a
teacher do to extend her classroom into the gymnasium? The following paragraphs do not contain new radical ideas for the teacher who has already
individualized learning in her classroom. Many of the suggestions are very
simple, but the experienced teacher will recognize that often the simplest
suggestions are the most effective.

Let us look at the types of situations that force a child to go beyond his
abilities, or those where the teacher removes the responsibility for safety from
the child to herself.

1. A situation arises where the whole class becomes so excited that something which originally was considered fun becomes uncontrolled and the
children end in having an accident or in tears. This often occurs in the

FIGURE 4.5   **FIGURE 4.6**

primary grades with running games of the chasing type. To stop this type of activity may sound as though we are trying to take all the fun out of the gymnasium. This is not the case; however, one must make sure that the type of activity is suitable to the maturity and experience of the children. For example, in a recent introductory activity, children had a band tucked in the back of their shorts, then ran all over the gymnasium floor trying to catch as many of the other children's bands or tails as possible without losing their own. One could see from their faces how much they enjoyed it. The activity, however, was not introduced until the children had been working in the gymnasium for about three months. If this game had been played before the children understood and had experienced safety training, there might well have been trouble and accidents.

2. Often the teacher can be overly concerned with the child's safety; hence, instead of creating situations where the children gradually learn to accept responsibility for their own safety, the teacher over-protects the children in order to make the gymnasium a "safe" place. For example, if children are arranged in lines for calisthenics, the spacing is often arrived at by putting the hands on the shoulders of the child in front. The child learns to reason that because he has done this, he is not likely to touch or bump into another child. Hence, in this type of formation he feels relieved of any responsibility. Another example of this over-protection is where children have been trained to run around the gymnasium in one direction only. Again, the *teacher* has taken the responsibility for their safety. She will say "run clockwise around the gymnasium," whereas, by telling them to "run anywhere in the gymnasium taking care not to collide" makes the child conscious that *he* has to be responsible. (Figure 4.7)

FIGURE 4.7

Kindergarten and First Grade children coming into the gymnasium for the first time do not naturally run in the same direction around the gymnasium. They run at different speeds because some are more physically mature and capable than others. It is interesting to watch how very few run fast at the start. This is not because they cannot go faster; it is because they are conscious that they may collide with someone else. Children who start by being allowed to run freely where the teacher emphasizes no collisions soon learn to run quickly and safely anywhere in the gymnasium. Furthermore, they will become more aware of available space and will not collide with other children or the apparatus.

Older children who have been conditioned to running around the gymnasium in one direction may take longer to adapt. This was particularly noticeable in a recent Grade Three class. It was apparent that they had little idea of how much space they needed to move in and how fast they could travel and still maintain control. Although they had lots of imagination and several good movement ideas they had many problems moving apparatus, and working without encroaching on another child's space. It was necessary to stress this side of safety training for a much longer period with this group.

3. Another potential danger is where the children are "spotted" or helped physically by the teacher or another classmate in performing a movement. Here part of the responsibility for safety is shifted from the performer to the spotter. Children should be taught to help one another but only *after* the child has first been taught to be responsible for his own personal safety. Few children are really physically capable of preventing a child from hurting himself. Needless to say it is also unfair to place a young child in such a position of responsibility.

4. Perhaps the most common cause of accidents is when the child is forced into attempting tasks beyond his present capabilities. This can happen

if the child feels he is letting his side down or thinks that it is the only way he can gain teacher approval. Not all children are physically capable of performing the same things simply because they are the same chronological age.

The Attitude of the Children

How then can a teacher inculate the attitudes of self-control, self-discipline, responsibility, and consideration? Perhaps the very first lesson in self-control for the child should be stopping and starting. This can be taught so that children enjoy it. Suitable activities will be found in the lesson plans for primary and intermediate grades. Keep the activities short and include lots of starting and stopping, but with all the children involved. The teacher must make sure when she says "stop," that she gets an immediate response. You may find children who try to take an extra turn. This must be discouraged as it is time wasted and unfair to other children. Usually, when working in groups the other children put on the necessary pressure to prevent a recurrence. Sharing and taking turns leads to self-control, and is usually stressed in the apparatus section of each lesson.

Self-discipline is fostered by allowing children to solve appropriate and meaningful problems. To enable this to take place the problems set by the teacher must be sufficiently broad to enable the least able as well as the skilled to find a solution.

Responsibility can be taught in many ways. A teacher must provide opportunities for each child to learn to run without colliding, to fall without hurting himself, and to carry apparatus carefully.

Consideration is linked so closely with responsibility it is often difficult to draw the line. Perhaps it is most easily shown in the sharing of equipment and movement ideas.

FIGURE 4.8   **FIGURE 4.9**

One word concerning working in bare feet and on hard surfaces without mats. Young children adapt to this very quickly and show sensitivity and careful handling of themselves when landing and rolling without mats. Older children take longer to adapt because of their previous experiences. Children and teachers are encouraged to work in bare feet where the surface of the floor makes it possible.

FIGURE 4.10   FIGURE 4.11

The authors have experienced all types of undesirable teaching situations and particularly where children rush into the gymnasium in a noisy uncontrolled fashion and with an attitude which precludes any form of genuine learning and teaching. The battle with this type of class may be long and uphill and heavier reliance has to be made upon more formal activities while attempting to inculcate desirable attitudes. On the other hand, many classes react well to the very first lesson taught with a Movement Education approach. It might be of interest to know, in the case of most of our student teachers who were introducing this approach in the various schools, the first three weeks were often spent battling noise, lack of sensitivity, and an indifferent attitude toward learning in the gymnasium. After this initial three-week period there was usually a transition to an enormously exciting atmosphere for both teacher and class. The children had become interested and challenged, hence accepted their new responsibilities. At the same time the student teacher began to see genuine spontaneity and creativity coming from the children.

So far we have said a great deal about the attitudes which are so necessary to ensure the safety of the children, but little on action, apart from running without colliding. The accompanying lessons will describe some ways to teach children to perform the safety sideways roll and how to land from heights. These are the main activities that are described in detail in the accompanying lesson plans.

The following lesson plans are suitable for any primary class which has not been in the gymnasium before, or for a class which has been conditioned to run in one direction in the gymnasium.

FIGURE 4.12   FIGURE 4.13   FIGURE 4.14

It should be realized that in the initial stages the average time for Kindergarten and Grade One to change into gymnasium clothes is almost twelve minutes. Grades Two and Three will take approximately eight minutes. However, this is not time wasted as they learn to tie shoes, fasten back buttons and many other tasks which, with practice, can be speeded up to three-four minutes for the whole class. Encourage children to ask their parents to time them when they get dressed in the morning. Also reward those who are quick to join into free play with balls or hoops, etc., until all are ready to begin the lesson.

Lesson No. 1

Part 1: Introductory Activity

Ask the children to run anywhere in the gymnasium without bumping into anyone and to stop quickly and stand very still when you say "stop," (Figures 4.13 and 4.14). Continue for three to four minutes. The purpose of this activity is to establish class control as the children must *listen* for your voice. Explain that sometimes you will say "stop" loudly while at other times you may speak very softly. Keep the interval between "stop" and "go" quite short (5-15 seconds) according to how sensibly they run. If the class does not respond quickly ask them to sit down instead of standing still when you say "stop" and make it a "musical bumps" game.

Teaching Points
1. Praise the first child you see who stops each time. This is the beginning of your observation.
2. Notice the child who is last to stop, only commenting if he improves, as "John was first to stop that time and Robert was much quicker than he was the last time."
3. Praise a child who does not collide and explain why she is good. Watch to see if any child repeatedly collides and if so make him walk until he has two turns without colliding.
4. Observe whether *all* the space of the gymnasium is being used. Are they running around the edge of the gymnasium leaving a great crater of space in the center? If so, ask the children to make zig-zag patterns with their feet as they run.
5. Emphasize good footwork. Running on balls of feet is essential in order to train the sensitivity in footwork which is a foundation of good movement, whether in games, gymnastics, or dance.
    "What!" you are saying, "All this in three minutes?" "Yes," we are saying, "but perhaps not all at once." In the first lesson it may be enough to accomplish just "stopping and starting" but suppose they are good at this, then check collisions, use of space, and footwork. Of course much will depend on each respective class. Nevertheless, as you will see in this introductory activity many things can be varied to keep the children's interest and, at the same time, will give the teacher an opportunity to emphasize these points. Bear in mind the purpose of the Introductory Activity is to provide a general warm-up period for the children, to establish class tone, and to stimulate interest.
6. If the children are better than you expected, let them know this. Also indicate that since they were so clever in stopping and starting you are going to look for two things, stopping and starting and *no* collisions. Then make it three adding space and zigzag floor patterns. Add this only when *real* progress is apparent.

General Comment
    To link this back to the explanation of safety training, the Introductory Activity first required the self-control to stop and start when told. Next we have borrowed twice from the space theme (see Chapter 6) by emphasizing running without colliding and running in zigzag patterns. Finally, we have borrowed from qualities (see Chapter 7) by requiring lightness of feet. All of these activities, however, specifically relate in a direct way to safety training.

Part II: Movement Training (approximately five minutes)

Ask the children to find a space of their own, and make sure it is big enough for them to lie down without touching anyone else. You must *look* to see that they are well spaced and, if necessary, ask children to move into larger spaces. Next, ask the class to make themselves very long and very thin. Some will stretch their arms above their heads, while others will not. Choose a child who is performing it with arms well extended and ask the others to sit up and observe the child's demonstration. Point out that the "demonstrator's" fingers are stretched as well as his toes.

FIGURE 4.15

Observe that most of the class will automatically lie on their backs to do this movement. Hence, ask them to try the same movement while lying on their stomachs. This will lead the class to the next stage which is "Roll on to your side and stay there. Next, roll on to your back, over to the other side, and back on to your tummy."

Children enjoy doing this and you can get them to change from tummies to backs as well as introduce left and right side at the same time. Now, allow them to roll across the floor for a very short time. Stop any child before he collides with another. In this instance, it is helpful to stand by two who are about to collide and ask the others to sit up and look. Ask them what would have happened if you hadn't said "stop." Can they think what these two should do? Some will say "roll the other way and in Grades Two or Three you may have one child who will say "find a larger space." If no child volunteers the answer you could say, "Instead of bumping, wouldn't it be fun to jump up and find another large space where you could start rolling again? Try that this time." Often you will find they will do this just for fun whether they are about to collide or not. Finally, make sure that they do not roll in one direction too long as they will become dizzy.

FIGURE 4.16

General Comments

Let us link this sideways roll to safety training and to future themes.

1. The children had to select a space large enough to lie down without touching anyone else. This is responsibility since they must make the initial decision.
2. We have borrowed a theme of "body awareness" (see Chapter 5) by stressing tummies, backs and sides, and stretching fingers and toes.
3. We have introduced rolling in the safety training theme.
4. We have repeated no collisions as in the introductory activity which requires self-control and self-discipline.

In later lessons we will be able to draw upon the "borrowed themes" by referring the children back, by saying to them "do you remember how you had to stretch for the log roll?"

Part III: Apparatus Work (approximately five minutes)

Tell the children to take a friend's hand and sit in a space anywhere in the gymnasium. Be quick to spot those who haven't a partner and join them in twos. Now, make four groups in the center allocating four or five pairs to each group according to class size. When in four groups explain that these will be their "section places" (or teams or homes) for apparatus work and they must remember where their places are and who is in their sections. Give them time to look and see who is in the same group. Then see if they can play the game of "section places." Here they can run, skip, or walk anywhere without colliding and when you say "section places" (or whatever term you wish to use), they run to their right places. (Figure 4.17)

In Kindergarten and Grade One this will require lots of practice. If the class can remember section places quickly and accurately three times in a

FIGURE 4.17

row, then let each section have a minute or two free play with small apparatus. Section places will be arranged as follows:

    Section one: A ball for each child
    Section two: A hoop for each child
    Section three: A beanbag for each child
    Section four: A skipping rope for each child

FIGURE 4.18

When you say "apparatus away, and back to your section places," each child must return his apparatus, then sit in his section place. Keep the storage box away from the wall and section places to allow for free circulation.

General Comments

The apparatus work is related to safety training in the following way:

1. Sitting with partner in a space requires cooperation and relates to the space theme.

2. Children begin to develop group responsibility for sharing apparatus, learning to take turns, and getting out apparatus. If a different child (or two) from each section puts the apparatus box into position and two other children put it away at the end of the period, this provides more opportunities for developing responsibility as well as self-confidence.

3. Remembering their groups encourages individual responsibility.

4. Each group working freely in one quarter of the gymnasium and not going into another group's space provides opportunities for practicing self-control and self-discipline.

5. Free play here entails working in a space by oneself without getting in another child's way, thus using freedom with consideration.

How much each teacher can do in the first lesson will, of course, depend upon the class. Some will be capable of doing *all* in the first lesson particularly at the Grade Three level; however, Kindergarten will need much practice, hence it will be unlikely that the latter will work on any apparatus in this lesson. It will be too difficult for these younger children to remember section places quickly enough. Also, they will be happy to play "section places" for much longer than would Grade Three children.

This is where we can only make suggestions. Each teacher must decide whether her class is ready to move on to a new challenge. If these children need more practice on a particular item, then you should choose another way of presenting the same material, still teaching and stressing the points you are trying to develop. You will soon learn which activities produce good results from your own class. Do not be afraid to try out your own variations as you go along.

This first lesson is based mostly on the direct and limitation teaching methods. The only indirect method came at the very beginning of the period where those who made a quick change were rewarded by having time to choose and play freely; and at the end, if there was time to go into actual apparatus work, to again play freely with the apparatus.

"How" you are saying "can I remember all this and teach at the same time?" The following *Lesson Reminders* should be used after you have studied the lesson. It provides a simple quick guide to use when you are teaching.

Lesson Reminder for Lesson No. 1

Free play with balls, beanbags, skipping ropes, and hoops for those who are quick in changing. Allow twelve minutes.

PART I: INTRODUCTORY ACTIVITY (3-4 minutes)
1. Class control—quick response.
2. No collisions—safety.
3. Spacing zigzag running—safety.
4. Footwork—quiet, light feet.

PART II: MOVEMENT TRAINING (Log rolls, 5 minutes maximum)
1. Find a space and lie down—spacing for safety.
2. Make yourselves very long and thin—stretch fingers and toes.
3. Roll—sides, backs, tummies, left and right.
4. Traveling rolling—stop before collision.
5. Jumping up and running into new space before rolling again.

PART III: APPARATUS WORK (5-6 minutes)
1. Choose partner and sit in a space. Look for odd children and pair off quickly.
2. Send pairs off to form four groups.
3. Play section places.
   Only if good enough, proceed to:
4. One or two children from each section to place box of equipment.
5. Free play with apparatus—stress no pushing.
6. Tidily and carefully put equipment away.
   Dressing twelve minutes. Faster ones could return boxes of apparatus to storage room, help slower ones to fasten back buttons, etc.

DIAGRAM A: Suggested Apparatus Arrangement for Lessons Nos. 1 and 2

Section 4: Beanbags	Section 2: Hoops
Section 3: Skipping ropes	Section 2: Balls

Lesson No. 2

Part I: Introductory Activity
Same as Lesson 1.

Part II: Movement Training
Same as Lesson 1.

Note: If you feel the children are ready to move to the next lesson without repeating Lesson No. 1, then begin your next lesson with Lesson No. 3.

Part III: Apparatus Work
If you feel the children are not sufficiently at ease moving to section places and working freely with one set of apparatus, repeat apparatus work for Lesson No. 1. In Lesson No. 2, you may rotate so that each section, after they have had a short turn with their apparatus, experiences playing with a different set. After each turn, the children should return equipment to the box, then return to section places. When everyone is sitting in their section places, tell Mary's section that they are going to play with beanbags in John's section place. With Kindergarten you may say "Let's watch and see if Mary's section can go to John's section place. Good, then come back again, and sit down. Now let's see if John's section can go to Bill's section place," etc., until all have practiced moving one place around. Emphasize no pushing, then let them have a short turn with their new apparatus. If possible allow the class to go to all four section places. They may not have too many ideas to start with for each piece of apparatus. At this stage you should be stressing safety, class organization, and freedom to choose for themselves. If they can work by themselves even for a short period, this is good—two minutes at each section is probably enough. Getting apparatus out of the box quickly and without fuss and putting it away is also important. Comments such as "Do you know in Grade One, John's section had much longer to play with their apparatus because they didn't push each other trying to get it" and "Bill's section was very quick at putting their apparatus away neatly so that it is ready for Mary's section to use," are particularly helpful at this stage.

Lesson Reminder for Lesson No. 2
Free play with beanbags, skipping ropes, and hoops for those who are quick in changing. Allow twelve minutes.

PART I: INTRODUCTORY ACTIVITY (Running and stopping, 2-3 minutes)
1. Class control.
2. No collisions.
3. Stress spacing, using all of the gymnasium and making zigzag patterns.
4. Footwork—quick light feet.

PART II: MOVEMENT TRAINING (Log rolls, 2-3 minutes. Shorter time to allow for more apparatus work)
1. Find a space and lie down—check spacing.
2. Make yourselves very long and very thin—stretch fingers and toes.
3. Rolling.
4. Traveling and jumping up into new spaces before collisions can occur.

PART III: APPARATUS WORK (Ten minutes)
1. Play "section places." If all in right places three times in a row, move to Sections.
2. Hoops, balls, skipping ropes, and beanbags.
3. Short turn at each section allowing approximately 1½ minutes each. This gives time to put apparatus back in box before moving to next section place.
4. At the end choose different children to put boxes away.
   Changing, allow twelve minutes.

Lesson No. 3

Part I: Introductory Activity

The emphasis here will be running and stopping, hiding elbows, knees, and noses. Before they start to run tell them which part of them they must hide when you say "stop."

FIGURE 4.19

You are still stressing the same safety ideas as in the first Introductory Activity, which are:
1. Quick response to "stop."
2. No collisions.
3. Sensible use of space, and

4. Good footwork. The teacher uses this Introductory Activity to lay the foundation for the sideways safety roll (which follows in Part II of this lesson) in a very simple fashion. It may be developed by posing the following questions:

    a. "Hide your nose this time when I say 'stop.'" Walk around and comment on those whose noses are really hidden.

    b. "This time I am going to make it more difficult. Noses were easy to hide, but as you run think how you can hide your knees when I say 'stop.'" Again walk around making sure all can do it. If not, select a child who is really hiding knees.

    c. "Good, this time it is going to be more difficult. I wonder who will be able to think of a really good way of hiding their elbows when I say 'stop.'"

       They usually find this the hardest to do. After they have had a try, select a child who tucks her elbows into her tummy, as this is the best position for the safety roll; ask them all to try it this way. Practice for two or three tries at each part.

    d. "Show me how clever you are; if you can hide all three—elbows, knees, and noses at the same time when I say 'stop.'"

FIGURE 4.20

This usually produces many giggles. Walk around and check that all parts are tucked in. It may be necessary to say "Michael, I can see your nose," or "Sally, your elbows are not tucked away," etc. You must *observe* what is going on so that you can help the children and prepare them for the next stage.

General Comments

We are borrowing from the "body awareness" theme by identifying certain parts, but again the stress is on safety.

FIGURE 4.21

Part II: Movement Training

Log and tucked sideways safety rolls (5-6 minutes). Continue posing questions:

1. "Is the space large enough for you to lie down and practice the log rolls as we did in the last lesson? If not, go into a bigger space and start practicing right away."

FIGURE 4.22

Let them have a short turn, remind them of the main points (see previous lesson). Give another short turn watching to see that they are not colliding and are using the space.

2. "Show me that you can still remember how to hide your nose, knees, and elbows all together. Now can you play the same game as log rolls, that is, jump up and run into a big space before you bump, but this time keep curled up tight into a little ball?"

Stress that elbows must be tucked into tummy and stay curled up tight. Select a child who does it well and get others to look and then try again. Explain why you thought it was good with comments such as

FIGURE 4.23

"her elbows are really tucked in"; she stays so tightly curled, just like a ball and can't possibly hurt her knees or elbows or nose"; "I think her secret must be that she keeps her nose on her knees, that is why she stays curled."

Most children will be able to do both log and tucked sideways rolls easily. However, it is important to stress the safety features. Some may complain at the start that they bump their elbows, so explain that this is why they must be tucked into tummies.

Part III: Apparatus Work

In this lesson Grades Two and Three should be ready to apply safety rolling to apparatus work. Use two benches and two large mats. Keep the balls and hoops for the other two sections and arrange as follows: (See lesson reminder for diagram of apparatus arrangement.)

1. Rolling hoop: (keeping in their quarter of the gymnasium).

   Try to go through it while moving, encourage rolling as soon as they go through.

FIGURE 4.24

FIGURE 4.25

2. Balls: Free play or gently moving ball along against tummy by doing log rolls and not letting ball travel too far (a ball of the size of a volleyball is best for this).
3. Benches: Traveling along bench by any method but landing with safety roll on floor. It is not necessary to have mats at end of bench but if you have more than two, use them. Moving benches is serious business. *Five* children to each bench for all primary grades, possibly more in Kindergarten and Grade One, and lay down firm rules. These are some suggestions:
   a. *Nobody lifts* bench until *all* are ready to lift.
   b. The child at either end must look to see that the rest have hands underneath bench ready to lift, (stress that *all* must help and be very strong).

FIGURE 4.26

   c. The two at the ends say "lift."
   d. One of the "ends" usually has to walk backwards. He must look over his shoulder to see where he is going and also the "end" who is walking forwards should also make sure that they will not walk into another group or piece of apparatus. The forward "end" should act as the pilot.
   e. When putting the bench down they should remind themselves and each other to keep their toes out of the way.
   f. The bench should be put down *carefully and quietly.*
   g. If not well done, make them put it back and get it out again, while groups who did it well get on with their work.
4. Large Mats: Any type of roll along mat. Encourage lots of quick turns. If the mats are the large (4 feet × 8 feet) then two children can roll across

each mat simultaneously. With some groups of Grades Two and Three (and this depends on individual classes) they can have a lot of fun and develop very good safety rolls by asking them to "faint" and as they flop onto the mat, turning their movement into a safety sideways roll. Another way is for them to deliberately trip up on the edge of the mat and then curl up and roll. This is one of the best ways of getting nearest to a "real-life" situation, and by stressing that hands and elbows must be tucked in and not touch the mat, the teacher can get the safety training across. Ask them to watch each other to see who tucks his hands in so they do not touch the mat.

General Comments

Remember that you must keep an eye on all four sections. Do not become so involved with one section that the others feel you have forgotten them. Some children find it more difficult than others to work by themselves; hence, the teacher should watch for those who need the extra boost until they can confidently work alone. Also, discipline problems will develop if you neglect the rest for one group, particularly in the beginning stages and if the class has been accustomed to a formal setting where they all did the same thing at the same time. At the same time cut short any type of silly behaviour. Kindergarten and Grade One adapt very quickly; however, children of this age level will tend to seek the center of attention by very obvious methods, hence, the teacher must tell the child to go back to her section place and work there and she will watch her from where she is standing. This simple technique makes them realize that the teacher does not have to be standing next to them to see what they are doing.

Most teachers will feel quite at ease with the Introductory Activity and Movement Training parts of the lesson but may feel out of their depth with the Apparatus section. This is a familiar feeling to all beginning teachers. For your own security, if you have enough equipment you may decide that you would feel more at ease if every child worked freely with the same type of apparatus. For example, if you have a class set of beanbags, divide the children into sections as in Lesson No. 1, then have four boxes of beanbags and proceed from there. Next lesson, if you have a class set of balls, let them work the same way. When you feel ready, have two groups using the one type of apparatus while the other two use a different type and gradually build towards four groups working with four different types of equipment.

Teachers, like children, learn at different rates; some can observe a wider range of activities more quickly than others and therefore can have only four different things going on but will be able to subdivide these four sections. The latter may be necessary when there is a limited amount of one type of apparatus. If children have something to work with, they soon learn to work independently and discipline problems usually disappear.

Lesson Reminder for Lesson No. 3

   Free play until all are ready with small apparatus (2-3 minutes).

PART I: INTRODUCTORY ACTIVITY (Running and stopping, hiding elbows, knees and noses)
1. Quick response.
2. No collisions.
3. Spacing.
4. Footwork.
5. Accurate "hiding" particularly of elbows, otherwise they will find the next part of lesson uncomfortable.

PART II: MOVEMENT TRAINING (Log and tucked sideways safety rolls, 5-6 minutes)
1. Short turn only at "logs."
2. Elbows, knees, and noses tucked in for sideways rolling. Emphasize elbows in.
3. Same game as for log rolls.

PART III: APPARATUS WORK (7-8 minutes)
1. Hoops—rolling, trying to go through and rolling.
2. Balls—free play or log rolling and pushing ball along as they roll.
3. Benches—traveling along by any method but getting off using safety roll.
   Take particular care in teaching handling of benches.
4. Mats—large or individual for quick turns at rolling, possible "fainting" or "tripping up" first.
   Time their changing and see if they have speeded up so that you can add any saved time to apparatus work in the next lesson.

DIAGRAM B: Suggested Apparatus Arrangement for Lesson No. 3

Section 4: Large and small mats	Section 1: Hoops
Section 3: Benches	Section 2: Balls

Lesson No. 4

Free play until all are ready. However, you may now like to suggest practicing rolls on the floor or mats. This period of time should be getting shorter, particularly with Grades Two and Three (ten minutes).

FIGURE 4.27

Part I: Introductory Activity (3-4 minutes)

Running and stopping making different parts *high,* such as elbows, knees, noses. If you choose knees first, this will help to get them started. Questions that will help to extend their movement experiences are:

1. "How can you make your elbows highest if you are lying down?" (On tummies or backs and get them to experience both.)
2. "How can you make your knees highest when you lie on your backs?"
3. "Can you do it with your nose too?"
4. "Now you choose one part of you, *not* nose, knees, or elbows and make that highest and we will guess which part you have chosen."

FIGURE 4.28

FIGURE 4.29

5. "Now work with your partner, one placing one part high and the other guessing, then change and give your partner a chance." Pick out interesting ones.

This activity borrows heavily for the theme "Increasing Range and Understanding of Movement," but is very necessary as the children are soon going to start to land and roll off apparatus from various heights. Knowledge and skill in this area increases their safety. It will still be necessary, however, to stress the safety factors of previous introductory activities.

Part II: Movement Training (5-6 minutes)

Having spent three lessons working on rolling, it is time to turn our attention to footwork for landing. This can be taught more effectively if the children work *without* shoes and socks. Begin by having them leap over beanbags, bands, individual mats, hoops, or whatever you have enough of to enable each child to jump over something. Stress landing big toe first, and bending the knees. A few quick turns and then work on "peeling" feet off floor, bit by bit, with the heels coming up first and big toe last. This will come if big toe leaves the floor last. Next have the children run and leap over beanbags (etc.) trying to land with the big toe first, bending ankles and knees as they land. Make sure they understand that by doing this they will not jar themselves when they land.

Part III: Apparatus Work From Section Places (6-8 minutes)

1. Skipping ropes: (one per child). Tying a knot in the rope by only using their feet, either standing up or sitting down. This is very good for keeping feet supple and strengthening the small foot muscles which are important for landing.
2. Hoops: One between two, hoop held horizontally about one foot off the ground by one child while another jumps into it and then wriggles out underneath without touching it. For those who can jump into the hoop held higher than one foot off the ground, encourage rolling out underneath.

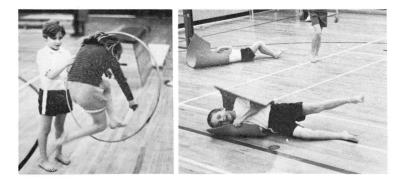

FIGURE 4.30

FIGURE 4.31

3. Mats: Individual or large mats. If the gymnasium has a stage and steps without a railing, the latter can be utilized for gradually increasing the height of the jump for landing and rolling. Children can select the height they feel most confident to jump from. Always make them start from the lowest even if they have one turn before going higher. Make sure their landings have "give" and elbows are tucked in when rolling. Do not allow too many children to wait for their turns. Use both ends of the stage or have four working on another mat away from the steps and four working from the steps. Rotate these children before shifting section places. Make sure that mats are carried by handles and not dragged.

4. Benches: Encourage running along broad side then jumping off and landing with "give" and rolling. Use as many benches as you have to give maximum number of turns. Reinforce "safety rules" for carrying benches. Also make sure each turn is quick and, at the same time, the mat is clear before each person starts his run and jump.

FIGURE 4.32   **FIGURE 4.33**

There will probably be only enough time in this lesson to work *one* section place. Nevertheless, train them to remember how many sections they cover each lesson (you should make a note yourself) so that time is not wasted in the next lesson while everyone tries to think where they finished in the previous lesson.

Lesson Reminder for Lesson No. 4

Changing time reduced to ten minutes for Grades Two and Three. Free play with small apparatus or practicing rolls.

PART I: INTRODUCTORY ACTIVITY (Three minutes)

Running, stopping—different parts high. Still stressing safety factors. Give opportunity for each child to select and provide an answer to the problem of stopping with one part highest.

PART II: MOVEMENT TRAINING (5-6 minutes)

1. Each child jumping over beanbag—landings.
2. "Peeling," work for stretch in ankles and suppleness of feet.
3. Running and leaping over any beanbag, stressing "give" in feet, ankles, and knees.

PART III: APPARATUS WORK

1. Skipping ropes—(one per child) tying knots using feet only. If successful, try tying bows.
2. Hoops—(one between two) held horizontally, jumping in and either wriggling or rolling out underneath.
3. Mats—large or individual and using stage steps if available; training in how to carry mats. Teach landings with roll from different heights.
4. Benches—running along, leaping, landing with "give" and rolling. Reinforce safety rules for carrying benches.
   Changing time 10 minutes.

DIAGRAM C: Suggested Apparatus Arrangement for Lesson No. 4

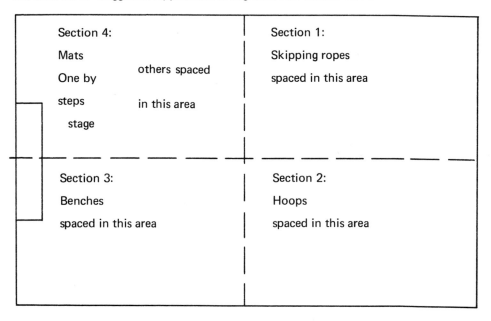

From now on no further reference will be made to time for changing at the beginning and end of lessons. On a two-lesson-a-week basis, with encouragement from classroom teachers and parents, it will take approximately twelve lessons before they can change in three or four minutes. Whether the teacher asks the children to practice specific tasks when they are ready or whether she allows them free choice will depend on the progress of the class. Free choice is desirable since it encourages the child to select his own apparatus and movement activities as well as to work independently. A specific task given by the teacher may be used to reinforce a technique or movement idea. For example "take out a beanbag and practice jumping over it, remembering to 'give' when you land." During this time the teacher can help individual children work at landings, and, at the same time, encourage the slower changers to be quicker. Psychologically this method has an interesting effect on the children. If the teacher stays close by the children until all are changed they are much slower than if she goes and works with the quick "changers." Encourage one child to undo another's back buttons rather than you doing it. As in all things a happy balance is required. Some children have difficulty in dressing when first coming to school and will become frustrated and sad at the beginning if left completely alone to manage by themselves; hence, the teacher should come back and give encouragement and help whenever necessary.

Lesson No. 5

Part I: Introductory Activity (2-3 minutes)

Running, leaping, landing, and rolling. Use the last part of the Movement Training of Lesson 4 and add rolling. You will find that most children will instinctively still put their hands out as they go to roll. We are attempting through this safety roll to prevent cut hands, grazed elbows, and broken wrists when children fall and tumble in out-of-school activities. This can be done by making a game out of being able to land and roll without hands touching the floor. Sometimes asking them to run with their arms folded will help the landing and rolling although it hampers their running and jumping.

FIGURE 4.34

Part II: Movement Training (4-5 minutes)

As you have seen, safety training depends on many other themes. We have now reached the stage where it is possible to move toward increasing the range and understanding of movement.

"Choose any way you can think of to travel across the floor *without* using your feet."

Pick out two or three different ideas and get each child to demonstrate, then allow the whole class to try the ideas. When selecting ideas try to find one child who is wriggling along on his tummy and using his hands. Find one who is on his back or is sitting and wriggling with his feet off the floor. The third should be a child who lies on her side. The teacher should now begin to make comments about each movement she observes and wishes to be demonstrated. For example, (1) "Look, Mary is on her tummy. Which part of her does she use to make herself travel? Yes, that's right, her hands." (2) "David is on his back and what does he use to move himself? Yes, just the upper part of his arms and elbows." (3) "Robert is on his side and observe how he travels; he bends and stretches all of himself, rather like a caterpillar." (4) "Jane was a clever girl, do you know what she did? Show them, Jane. Yes, a log roll, and she is right, isn't she? She is not using her feet to travel at all."

We have used some of the children's ideas to extend their range of movement by asking them to travel, taking their weight on just hands and knees or hands and feet. The latter has many different varieties which can be drawn out of the children. For example, children can move with either face down or face up, and legs can be straight or bent. They may travel forwards, backwards, or sideways. Other different types of movement could be elbows and seats, backwards, forwards, or sideways. Ask the children to think up movements that have not been used and ask them to demonstrate. Remember to pose each movement task in words rather than by a demonstration of the type of movement desired. This technique will help the children to think of different ways of fulfilling the task since you have not given them a visual image.

Part III: Apparatus Work

Same as previous lesson.

In the primary grades, changing for the first few weeks takes up a lot of the lesson time, hence apparatus time is short. However, freedom from clothing, learning safety factors such as taking care of themselves and of the apparatus, cannot be stressed too much. Young children enjoy being helpful and being made responsible for certain tasks. Hence, the standards you set in these early stages are most important. High standards set now will save time, temper, and equipment throughout the rest of the year. Furthermore, much of this training is applied to the apparatus part of the lesson. Do not accept banging down of benches from any grade level. All are capable of lifting and carrying benches carefully and quietly. Do not accept mats being dragged across the floor. Do not allow beanbags, hoops, or balls to remain all over the floor.

Other possible variations in apparatus work for safety training are listed below. Obviously you will use as much of what is available and substitute wherever it may seem necessary.

1. Wall bars. Start jumping off lowest rung, landing and rolling either with or without mats, and increasing the challenge by going up one rung each time. Emphasis on landing and rolling.

FIGURE 4.35

2. Ropes tied through benches. Start by having bench one foot off the ground at one end, and increase the height as they become more skilled. Emphasis on landing a n d rolling (Figure 4.37).

3. Top section of vaulting box. Any method of getting on to the box but landing and rolling (Figure 4.35).

FIGURE 4.36

4. Storming. Two benches inclined and hooked on to a third bench turned balance side up and at right angles to other two.
5. Ropes. Swinging and landing backwards going into backward diagonal roll. This should be done only after the backward diagonal roll has been taught.
6. Three bamboo canes balanced on chairs or small wooden 9″ blocks. Leaping over, landing and rolling. (See Figure 4.36)

Lesson Reminder (1) for Lesson No. 5

PART I: INTRODUCTORY ACTIVITY

Running and leaping, landing and rolling. Emphasis on tucking in hands and elbows in preparation for rolling.

PART II: MOVEMENT TRAINING (4-5 minutes)

Choose any way you can think of to travel across the floor without using your feet.

Select three or four ideas pointing out how one differs from the other and which parts are bearing weight. Also which parts are used for propelling themselves along.

Then ask them to travel (1) hands and knees
                        (2) hands and feet
                        (3) elbows and seats
                        (4) you think up a method

PART III: APPARATUS WORK

1. Skipping ropes—tying knots or bows.
2. Hoops—leaping in and wriggling or rolling out.
3. Mats and stage—jumping, landing and rolling.
4. Benches—running along, leaping off, landing and rolling.

FIGURE 4.37

DIAGRAM D: Suggested Apparatus Arrangement for Lesson No. 5

Section 4: 3 benches for storming	Section 3: Vaulting Box	Section 7: Hoops	Section 1: Wall bars and mats
Section 2: Climbing ropes tied to support the inclined benches OR mats and stage	Section 5: Climbing ropes	Section 8: skipping ropes	Section 6: 3 bamboo canes wooden blocks or chairs

Lesson Reminder (2) for Lesson No. 5

PART I: INTRODUCTORY ACTIVITY

Running and turning in the air landing and sideways rolling.

PART II: MOVEMENT TRAINING

Suitable for Grades Two and Three if individual mats are available, place two end to end.

1. Child A lies in log position at end *off* the mat. Child B runs, leaps over Child A, lands and rolls. Change over.
2. Variations of this can be that Child A forms tucked roll position, this means Child B will have to jump higher so use this as first progression.

FIGURE 4.38

3. Child A lies at far end of mat and starts log rolling along mat towards Child B who then runs and jumps over while A is still rolling. B finishes with a roll as before.

PART III: APPARATUS WORK

Ask the children to work in sub-sections (four or five) and make up sequences of jumping over and rolling. Any section which thinks up a good pattern can show the other who then can copy. The teacher circulates and should be ready with suggestions such as "could two of you roll holding wrists while the other two jump over?"

FIGURE 4.39

Ask them to make sure that in their sequence each person has a turn at rolling and also a turn at jumping.

Teachers can build up longer sequences by selecting different ideas from different groups and making one lead into another.

The five previous lesson plans will give the basis for safety training. Before moving to the next theme the teacher must decide whether the following has been accomplished.

1. The class stops quickly when told and listens for instructions.
2. The noise level is such that the teacher's voice can be heard.
3. The children understand moving in a space, traveling in different directions without colliding, and can do a sideways safety roll on landing.
4. The children can work independently within a group.
5. The children can move apparatus carefully and efficiently.
6. The children show care and consideration for others' needs.

If she feels that she is satisfied with the standards her class has reached then they will be ready to go on to the next stage. However, some classes will need more than five lessons to reach this stage, in which case the teacher may repeat any of the lessons and/or try to invent variations of those suggested here, putting special emphasis on her class's particular needs.

DIAGRAM E: Suggested Apparatus Arrangement for Lesson No. 5 (2)

Section 4b:	Section 4a:	Section 1b:	Section 1:
Four or five individual mats or working on bare floor	Large mat	Four or five individual mats or working on bare floor	Large mat
Section 3b:	Section 3a:	Section 2b:	Section 2a:
Large mat	Four or five individual mats or working on bare floor	Large mat	Four or five individual mats or working on bare floor

CHAPTER

FIVE

Theme Two:
Adding to the Range
and Understanding
of Movement

It should now become apparent that safety training depends on the child's knowledge of his own abilities and limitations. The teacher's task is to assist each child to add to his knowledge of movement patterns and to improve his physical skills in progressive stages. By gradually increasing a child's range of understanding and movement, he, in turn, is able to take more and more responsibility for his own safety.

FIGURE 5.1

Lesson No. 1

Part I: Introductory Activity

Running and stopping with weight on different parts of the body. For example, stopping on two feet, left foot, right foot, one hand and one foot, back, stomach, seat, shoulders, elbows and knees, and knee of one leg and toes of other foot.

This can be as easy or as difficult as you wish to make it. Since Kindergartens and Grades One may have problems with left and right, this is a good beginning activity for them. Always give at least one opportunity to choose which part(s) they put their weight on.

Part II: Movement Training

Individual mats are on the floor for backward diagonal roll. Set a movement task such as: put weight on feet, seat, shoulders, seat, then feet. This should produce a backward rock. Once they have discovered this, get them to start with a little backward rock, hugging their knees, then a bigger one, and finally a bigger one still.

"Now this time when you do your biggest rock backward can you put *both* knees by your *right* ear?" Then repeat doing left ear. Many children will put one knee by each ear. Get a child to demonstrate and point out that both knees are by one ear. Allow several practice turns.

"This time when you do your biggest rock backwards, see if you can go right over and land on both knees." Stress putting knees down gently.

FIGURE 5.2

Part III: Apparatus Work

1. Eight or nine bowling pins for the group and a ball for each child. Dribbling the ball in and out without getting in each other's way and without knocking the pins down. All should practice at the same time. Initially, pins can be arranged without any definite shape or pattern and with lots of room between each pin. As skill increases move the pins closer together.

FIGURE 5.3

2. Hoops and Beanbags: (one per each child) Invent as many different ways as you can of picking up the beanbag with different parts of the body and then throwing it into the hoop. Ask each child to invent three different ways and to practice until he can do them well.

3. Benches or Box: Traveling backward along bench, jumping off backward and doing backward diagonal roll on landing.

FIGURE 5.4

4. Large Mats and Stage: Using the stage, jumping off steps backward starting from bottom and working upward using backward roll for landing.

5. Climbing Ropes: Swinging on ropes, landing backward and rolling. Here the emphasis is on safety. The first time the ropes are used have the whole class sit near the ropes so that you can explain the important safety precautions.

Make sure all children sit in front or behind ropes and not in the downward path of where the ropes would swing out if not properly controlled. The teacher may forcefully swing a rope so that children can see how easily they could get hurt if they were in the way. One demonstration of this is a very effective way of driving this point home and usually the children are very impressed. This will also save you hours of saying "don't stand in the way of the ropes."

Ropes fascinate children, hence make sure that all have a chance to try them before they are put away. Stress the need for strength and lots of practice. Allow free practice on the ropes, and stay by this section. Constantly stress coming down "hand over hand" *not* sliding because the latter causes friction, burns and accidents.

FIGURE 5.5   FIGURE 5.6

Do not allow any child to swing off the stage or anything else that will give them height. Even if children run on the floor and reach up as high as they can, they will not swing with the same momentum as they would from a height, and there will be no danger of falling.

Always drop off the rope when *swinging backward when the rope reaches the highest point of its swing.* The rope almost stops before beginning its forward swing—this is the best time to drop off and do a backward or sideways roll—the rope will swing forward away from the child as she drops.

A helpful suggestion for Grade One and Kindergarten is to stand at the bottom of the rope, jump up, keeping arms bent and making the chin stay on the hands. Set "count tasks" until they can hold this position for the count of ten or more.

FIGURE 5.7

FIGURE 5.8

Lesson Reminder for Lesson No. 1

PART I: INTRODUCTORY ACTIVITY
Running stopping weight on different parts.

PART II: MOVEMENT TRAINING
Individual mats on floor for backward diagonal roll. Problem: feet-seat-back-shoulder-back-seat-feet. The little rock, bigger rock, and a huge one. Two knees by right ear (or left). Knees down gently.

PART III: APPARATUS WORK
1. Eight or nine pins for group and a ball for each child (dribbling for good footwork).
2. Hoops and beanbags—Picking up beanbag with different parts and throwing it into the hoops.
3. Benches—Traveling backward and jump off backward into a diagonal roll.
4. Large or individual mats, and stage for backward jumps and rolls.
5. Swinging on ropes.
6. Skipping ropes for tying knots or bows.
7. Two sections of box, getting on without using hands, jump, land and roll off.

DIAGRAM F: Suggested Apparatus Arrangement for Lesson No. 1

Section 4:	Section 7:	Section 1:	Section 6:
space	Box: two	8 or 9	Skipping ropes
other	sections	pins	for tying knots
Mat and stage mats			
Section 3:	Section 5:	Section 2:	
4 Benches	Swinging on ropes	Hoops and beanbags	

Lesson No. 2

Part I: Introductory Activity

Running keeping on tiptoes, "What other parts of your feet can you use to walk on?" (heels, sides, etc.) Make up a pattern using three movements such as forward on tiptoes, backward on heels, and sideways crossing one foot over the other and keeping on side. Try to pick out a child's idea that shows different ways and have the whole class practice it.

Part II: Movement Training

Working with partner and a ball. Begin by "shooting feet," sitting with legs straight, and backs of knees against floor. Take imaginary pistols from pockets and use feet as targets, toes sticking up until "shot at," then keeping legs straight, stretching toes down toward ground. (Back of knees must touch the floor at all times.) Start by "shooting" both together, then one at a time, seeing who can make big toes touch the ground while backs of knees still against ground. Next, partners watch each other jump and land. Remember: pointed toes, stretched ankles, and good "gives" on landing.

FIGURE 5.9   FIGURE 5.10

Part III: Apparatus Work

1. Ropes: Swinging, now stress bent arms and feet and legs stretched and straight during swing.

FIGURE 5.11

2. Balls: Catapulting balls against the wall with feet, chasing them as they bounce off and "re-fire."
3. Box: Getting over, across along without putting feet on top of box. Roll on landing.

FIGURE 5.12

4. Hoops and bags: Same as previous lesson.
5. Benches: Same as previous lesson.
6. Large or individual mats and stage. Same as previous lesson.

Lesson Reminder for Lesson No. 2

PART I: INTRODUCTORY ACTIVITY
   Running on tiptoes, walking on heels, sides of feet; pattern using all three.

PART II: MOVEMENT TRAINING
1. "Shooting feet."
2. Catapulting ball between two using feet.
3. Watching partner jump and land. Stretch legs, ankles, toes; "give."

PART III: APPARATUS WORK
1. Ropes swinging—bent arms, stretched feet and safety rules.
2. Catapulting balls against wall, stressing action of toes to get force.
3. Box—getting over, across, along without putting feet on box. Roll on landing.
4. Hoops and beanbags as before.
5. Benches as before.
6. Large mats and stage as before.

Lesson No. 3

Part I: Introductory Activity

Running and stopping. This time they should run with two parts of the body touching the floor, (two feet). "Can you now run with four parts on the ground?" (both hands and both feet). "Now try three." Keep turns short as this is tiring, and alternate running with the other two types.

FIGURE 5.13

Part II: Movement Training

Individual mats on floor. Use a beanbag and pose the following questions:
1. "Can you take your weight on two hands and one foot?"
2. "Now stretch the leg in the air, can you make it straighter?"
3. "Are your toes really stretched?"
4. "Now let's try with the other leg in the air."
5. "Can you do the same thing again but hold a beanbag against your chest with your chin?" (See Figure 5.14)

Next stage make knee of supporting leg touch beanbag at same time as chin. By slowly straightening the leg in the air most of the children will

FIGURE 5.14

go into forward roll. Keep the chin firmly on beanbag as this prevents any weight going on to head and also keeps the backs rounded. Supporting knee on beanbag keeps back rounded, and lifting the other leg allows for control of speed.

Allow those who are hesitant to do it on a mat. Never force a child over. The forward roll is harder than the log, sideways tucked or backward diagonal roll, and children may need more time to feel confident enough to try to go right over.

Part III: Apparatus Work

Include one section where individual mats or a large mat can be used so children can invent different types of forward rolls while holding beanbags with different parts of the body.

FIGURE 5.15

The rest of the apparatus work will be the same as in the previous lesson. Remember that safety of children in handling themselves and equipment will still need attention. By this time even the youngest children should be able to do the log, sideways, backward diagonal rolls. Many children will be able to do the forward roll. All should be able to move confidently in the gymnasium, be able to use space, and work independently with small apparatus. They should be able to go to "section places" quickly and co-operate when getting out large apparatus. Selecting and choosing apparatus, however, will require additional assistance.

Additional Teaching Points

1. At least one section should have a direct link with the movement training part of the lesson.
2. Keep apparatus in the same position until every section has had a chance to use it. In subsequent plans it is suggested that apparatus activities

should tie in with the lesson plans, that as large a variety of apparatus as possible should be used, and that selection should be possible. Never be afraid to improvise.

3. Always include one section in which children have freedom to invent and combine ideas. Children in Grades Two and Three will often produce excellent ideas when working with their friends.

4. Make sure that you observe each child during apparatus work. If there is only time for the children to work at one section then the teacher should go around to each section. However, if there is time for them to move to all four, the teacher may want to teach or see that each child understands one particular point, in which case she should stay at that section and let each group come to her.

5. Remember to use the time profitably at the beginning, while the children are changing.

6. We have not mentioned using the large climbing apparatus such as the Southampton Cave,[1] etc., since many schools do not have this equipment. However, if available this apparatus can be used from the very beginning and provides excellent opportunities for safety training. Children in Kindergarten and Grade One can handle this apparatus very easily and love to do so. (See Figures 5.16, 5.17 and 5.18)

FIGURE 5.16

---

[1]Cave or C.A.V.E. refers to climbing and vaulting equipment.

FIGURE 5.17

FIGURE 5.18

Lesson Reminder for Lesson No. 3

PART I: INTRODUCTORY ACTIVITY

Running, stopping, two, three, and four parts on ground.

PART II: MOVEMENT TRAINING

For forward rolls on individual mats or floor.
1. Weight on two hands and one foot.
2. Stretch other leg in air.
3. Try other leg.
4. Hold beanbag to chest with chin.
5. Add touching knee to beanbag.
6. Slowly stretch free leg up and then they will gently roll over.

PART III: APPARATUS WORK
1. Individual mats and beanbags.
2. Ropes for swinging.
3. Catapulting balls against the wall.
4. Box—two layers—over, across, along without using feet on top, but roll on landing.
5. Picking up beanbags with different parts and throwing through hoop.
6. On benches either broad or balance, side, off, roll on landing.
7. Large mats and stage for landing and rolling.

Lesson No. 4

Note: the following lesson is a suggested plan for all children using the same type of apparatus.

Part I: Introductory Activity

Place one hoop for each child on the floor. Ask the children to run freely and then to stop at any hoop. The teacher should explain to the children just *before* they run which part of their bodies to put into the hoop when she says "stop." Choose easy parts first, for example, one foot, knees, hand(s), then progress to the more difficult, (elbow, shoulders, seats, backs, tummies, etc.). Make the last turn sitting in the hoop so that they are ready for movement training.

FIGURE 5.19

Part II: Movement Training

Each child working with one hoop. Ask them to get over their hoop without touching it. Observe whether they took a one or two foot takeoff, or whether any child traveled over his hoop without jumping. Next ask the children to jump over their hoops and land on one foot, then on two feet. Finally allow the class to practice any other way that may appeal to them.

FIGURE 5.20

The next movement task is to go around their hoops without touching them. Pose a question, "I wonder who is going to be first to think of a way?" Select the first child you see who fulfills the task and have him demonstrate, then ask the others to see if they can go around their hoops in a different way. Observe:

1. How many run around,
2. How many put one foot in the middle of the hoop and the other outside and run around,
3. Anyone who used hands and feet, or
4. Both feet in and both hands out, or
5. Feet out and hands in, or
6. One of each on either side.

FIGURE 5.21

FIGURE 5.22

There are many possible variations here. If the children do not think of them, pose questions such as "Who can make his feet go around his hoop while keeping his hands in the middle of the hoop?" This will help the children solve their problems without always having a visual demonstration. It is most important for them to learn to work out instructions from words as it makes them think, thus increasing their independence, initiative, and creativity. However, children should not be allowed to flounder. If a large number of the children cannot think of a solution and do not start to work quickly, have a child demonstrate who has thought of a solution. It is extremely unlikely in the primary grades that this particular type of lesson will create any difficulty. Nevertheless, it is well to know how to handle the problem should it occur. Another way is to rephrase the question.

If you then asked the class to go across from one side of the hoop to the other the children may perform bunny jumps, handstands, or cartwheels, all of which are suitable responses to the question. Some, however, may not be able to think of a way. In this case ask them to put their hands on the floor in the middle of the hoop and move their feet from one side of the hoop to the other. This will make the task simple for them to follow but does not allow too much scope for individual ideas.

Next, ask the children to touch the hoop with as many parts of their bodies as they can. Observe:

FIGURE 5.23

1. Seat, two hands and two feet, or
2. Hands, elbows, knees, feet, and nose, or
3. Lying around edge of hoop either with tummy touching, or
4. Alternately back touching, or
5. Lying side touching the hoop.

Select children showing these variations and then ask the remainder of the class to try each idea in turn, making it clear which parts of their body should be touching the hoop.

Part III: Apparatus Work

Note: Continue with hoop work. Pose the following movement tasks:

1. Touch or hold your hoop with four parts.
2. Touch or hold your hoop with three parts.
3. Touch or hold your hoop with two parts.
4. Now only one part.

FIGURE 5.24

FIGURE 5.25

FIGURE 5.26

Explain to the children they now can build a sequence using the ideas the class produced. You should give a very simple example, such as, "with the hoop on the floor, both hands and both feet touching the edge of the hoop, make a bridge shape with tummy upwards. Now turn over so that tummy is downwards and balance on two hands and one foot. Next turn sideways so that one hand and one foot are on the hoop, finally stand up and balance hoop on top of head and climb through." Make changes from one to the next as smooth as possible.

Lesson Reminder for Lesson No. 4

PART I: INTRODUCTORY ACTIVITY

Hoops scattered over the floor. Running and stopping with different parts in hoop.

PART II: MOVEMENT TRAINING

"Get over your hoop without touching it." Observe:

1. One foot takeoff.
2. Two foot takeoff.
3. Any other method.

"Go around your hoop without touching it." Observe:

1. Running around edge.
2. One foot in middle pivoting while other foot outside hoop.
3. Hands and feet, both in and out or on either side.

"Touch the hoop with as many parts of you as you can." Observe:

1. Seat, two hands, two feet.
2. Hands, elbows, knees, feet, and nose.
3. Lying around edge, tummy touching.
4. Back touching.
5. Side touching.

PART III: APPARATUS WORK

Build sequence from classes' ideas using 4, 3, 2, 1 parts of body touching or holding hoop.

Lesson No. 5

Part I: Introductory Activity

Scatter individual mats or beanbags over the gymnasium floor (one per child). Ask the children to run and stop, and balance on different parts of their bodies. (Example: 2 feet, 1 foot, hand and 1 knee, 2 knees, seat, shoulders, tummy, nose and knees, elbows and or on heels.) Since this is free choice,

FIGURE 5.27

you will often see headstands and handstands appear from the more able students. The teacher should always give the children an opportunity to think for themselves and to choose an activity which is personally challenging.

Part II: Movement Training

Ask the children to lie on the mat touching it with as much of their bodies as they can. Next change the emphasis by challenging them to make as little of their bodies touch the mat as possible. Observe:
1. Toe of one foot, or
2. One knee, or
3. One heel, etc.

Now, challenge them to think of as many different ways as they can to go over their mats. Observe:
1. Leaping with a one foot take off, or
2. Jumping with a two foot take off, or
3. Leaping with a turn, landing and rolling, etc.

Following this, see if they can touch the mat with one part of their bodies and make their feet travel all around the edge. Observe:
1. One hand, or
2. Elbow, or
3. Seat

Part III: Apparatus Work

Note: continue working on individual mats.

This is the beginning of cartwheels. Pose the following movement tasks and questions:
1. Two hands in the middle of mat and jump, moving feet from side to side. Allow several practices.

FIGURE 5.28

2. Now start from standing position and repeat (1) and end in a standing position. Next *without* turning around come back to original side. Again allow several practices.

FIGURE 5.29

3. From a standing position place one hand on the mat and then the other and move feet across and right back to original side without turning. This helps a child to discover which hand he prefers as well as making him practice with each hand at this early stage.

FIGURE 5.30

At this point many children will be doing some form of cartwheels. This is where one should also stress quality by having the children begin to focus their attention on what happens to their legs when they are upside down. For those who are producing a type of cartwheel, questions such as, "Can you stretch up so that your feet almost brush the ceiling?" or "Are your knees straight?" will direct the children's attention to using different parts in different ways. For the majority of the children, however, the emphasis will be on getting one leg high in the air. This is the turning "inside-out" stage. Let them choose which hand they prefer to put down first. Follow this with a slow motion movement of putting the second hand down. Next, first foot and turning so that by putting the second foot down they end up by facing the same direction they started from.

This is where the teacher is able to give individual help to those who are finding it difficult. Ask these children to bring their mats to one part of the gymnasium while the others either practice by themselves on the shape of their cartwheel or with a partner work on making a pattern of cartwheels. Grade Three children work well together on patterns if you suggest that they fill in all sides of a square or go around together.

Lesson Reminder for Lesson No. 5

PART I: INTRODUCTORY ACTIVITY

Mats. Running and stopping balancing on different parts. Tell them each time *before* they run.

PART II: MOVEMENT TRAINING

"Lie on the mat touching it with as much of you as you can." "Now as little of you on the mat as possible."
1. Tip toe on one foot.
2. One knee.
3. One heel, etc.
   "Think as many ways as you can to go *over* your mat."
1. Leaping one foot takeoff.
2. Jumping two foot takeoff.
3. Leaping with turn landing and rolling, etc.
   "Touch the mat with one part of you and make your feet travel all around the edge."
1. One hand.
2. Elbow.
3. Seat, etc.

PART III: APPARATUS WORK

Cartwheels across individual mats.
1. Two hands, jump feet across.
2. Standing, then two hands, jump feet across and stand.
3. Standing, one hand, second hand, jumping feet across, stand.
4. Standing, one hand, second hand, one leg high and then stand.
5. Turning inside out.
6. More help for individuals, patterns for those who are ready.

Lesson No. 6

Part I: Introductory Activity

Children scattered on the floor, each with one beanbag. They should run, stop and freeze *without moving* their *feet*. From this position they must reach out to the nearest beanbag; touch it with a part of their body that was selected by the teacher. To prevent children from trying to stop very close to a beanbag and therefore preventing another child from being able to use it, vary the parts, such as head, nose, and ears. The latter are hard to accomplish if they have stopped too close to the beanbag. We often call this type of game "nine lives" so that each time they are too far from a beanbag and cannot reach and touch the right part of their body they lose a "life." They must keep track of their own "lives." This is good training in being a good loser and not cheating. Don't expect perfect results.

FIGURE 5.31

Part II: Movement Training

Beanbag in a space for each child.

Pose the question "How many different ways can you pick up the beanbag?" Observe:

FIGURE 5.32

1. Fingers,
2. Toes,
3. Teeth,
4. Trapping between elbow joint,
5. Trapping between the knee joint,
6. Both feet,
7. Both knees, or
8. Chin against chest.

Next, "Can you throw the beanbag into the air one way and catch it a different way?" Observe:

1. Pick up with toes, throw to hands.
2. Pick up with teeth, throw to feet or knees.
3. Pick up with one hand, throw to other.

Next, "Put the beanbag behind your heels, now without turning around can you pick it up with your hands and toss it over your head so that it lands on the floor in front of you?" "Can you, in one jump, land in front of the beanbag and then toss it over your head?" (Figure 5.34)

This is a useful activity for teaching the children the safe hand position needed for backward roll on the ropes and reverse hanging on the wall bars.

FIGURE 5.33

FIGURE 5.34

FIGURE 5.35

This could be included where wall bars or ropes are used in the apparatus section of another lesson.

"Shaggy Dog." "Kneel on all fours and put the beanbag on your back, keeping arms straight, wiggle, and toss it off." Some of the children may be familiar with "humping and hollowing" the back which is a good activity for developing mobility of the spines. (Figure 5.35)

Part III: Apparatus Work

Note: Continue working with the beanbags.

Free practice of anything in the lesson or any new ideas with a partner or alone. If they run out of ideas, suggest:

1. Sitting, picking beanbag up with feet, rocking backward and trying to put it down on the floor over their heads.
2. With both hands on floor and beanbag between feet, jump, raising both feet into the air and toss the beanbag over their head, or
3. Have all of the class try out some of the children's inventions.

Lesson Reminder for Lesson No. 6

PART I: INTRODUCTORY ACTIVITY

Beanbags scattered. Running and stopping, freezing feet; then reaching out to touch beanbag with different parts of body.

PART II: MOVEMENT TRAINING

"How many ways can you pick up the beanbag?"

Let them try each other's ideas, use above list if you cannot find six or seven different ways from the children's list of ideas.

"Can you throw the beanbag into the air one way and catch it a different way?"

1. Feet to hands.
2. One hand to other.
3. Teeth to hands, feet, or knees.

"Put beanbag behind heels, without turning around, bend and pick it up with hands, toss it over head."

Now jump forward over the beanbag and start again.

"Shaggy Dog."

PART III: APPARATUS WORK

Free practice of anything in the lesson or any new ideas. Suggestions for those who run out of ideas:

1. Sitting, beanbag between feet, rock backwards and put bag down over head.
2. Both hands on floor, beanbag between feet, jump feet in air trying to toss beanbag over head, or
3. Get whole class to try out some of the children's inventions.

Lesson No. 7

Part I: Introductory Activity

Free play with balls. (Balls should be 5" or larger, and one for each child.)

FIGURE 5.36

Part II: Movement Training

"How many times can you bounce it with your hand?" Allow several turns.

"Can you bounce it first with one hand and then with the other?" Allow several turns.

"Now bounce it once and then catch it." Repeat several times.

"Can you run, bounce, and catch?" Children of Grades Two and Three should be able to, while Kindergarten and Grade One will need lots of practice.

"Throw the ball up, let it bounce, and then catch it." "Can you invent a trick to do while the ball is in the air?"

1. Clap hands.
2. Turn around, etc.

"Try rolling it along on floor hard and fast so that it hits the wall and bounces back—can you catch it?"

"Throw it against the wall and catch it." Some will find it easier to let the ball bounce first.

"Can you invent a trick to do before you catch the ball?" Observe:

1. Clap hands.
2. Turn around, or
3. Sit down and get up again or catch it sitting down.

"Kick the ball against the wall hard and then catch it as it comes back with your hands."

Part III: Apparatus Work

Note: Continue with ball work.

Section 1: Working in twos. "Invent as many different ways as you can think to throw the ball against the wall for your partner to catch." (1. standing, 2. sitting, 3. kneeling)

Section 2: Working in twos. Throwing the ball into the basketball hoop and partner chasing it. This is an activity that Kindergarten children instinctively try and they enjoy running after their particular ball. There is usually great excitement if they hit the ring or net, and ecstasy if it goes through.

Section 3: Working in twos, one throwing ball against wall finding a way to jump over it as it bounces, partner catches and then it is her turn to throw and jump. Some will try forward and others backward and one or two may spin the whole way around.

Section 4: "Pig in the middle" done by rolling ball along floor if not sufficiently skilled to do throwing and catching.

Lesson Reminder for Lesson No. 7

PART I: INTRODUCTORY ACTIVITY
    Free play with balls.

PART II: MOVEMENT TRAINING
 1. Bouncing with one hand.
 2. Bouncing alternating hands.
 3. Bounce and catch.
 4. Bounce and catch on the run.
 5. Throwing the ball up, let it bounce, and then catch.
 6. Invent a "trick" to do while the ball is in the air.
 7. Roll hard against wall and catch it as it bounces back.
 8. Throw against wall and catch.
 9. Invent a "trick."
 10. Kick the ball against the wall, catch with hand.

PART III: APPARATUS WORK
Section 1: Throw different ways against wall for partner to catch.
Section 2: Throw into basketball nets, partner chasing it and then having a turn.
Section 3: Throw against wall; invent a jump over ball as it bounces; partner catches and then has a turn.
Section 4: Pig in the middle—vary according to ability.

Lesson No. 8

Part I: Introductory Activity
    Skipping ropes for each child. Skipping either on the spot or traveling. Kindergarten and Grade One will not find this easy so an alternative for them would be to put skipping rope on the floor and have them running and jumping as many times as they can before you say "stop."

Part II: Movement Training

Each child should be in his own space. Tell the class to put the rope in a straight line.

1. "Can you walk along the rope?"
2. "Can you jump from side to side along the rope?"
3. "Can you do ten jumps before you get to the end?"
4. "Can you do them very quickly?"
5. "Can you do them backwards?"
6. "Can you make a bridge over your rope?"
7. "How many different ways can you travel as a bridge over your rope?"

FIGURE 5.37   FIGURE 5.38

FIGURE 5.39   FIGURE 5.40

The teacher now selects one method standing up, one with hands and feet on floor, and one with knees on floor. Ask the class to practice all three and then ask them to add one of their own so that the sequence will contain four different ways of traveling along rope.

Part III: Apparatus Work

Section 1: Join up with partner and use only one rope for each pair; invent different ways of skipping with each child holding one end of rope, then with one child holding both ends of rope.

Section 2: Working on own:
  a. Skipping on one foot only
  b. Changing feet.
  c. Both feet together very quickly.
  d. Backwards.
  e. Arms crossing.

Section 3: With partner and rope on floor, invent jumping pattern using hopping on one foot, jumping with feet apart and also feet together; starting positions can be from opposite ends of rope, side by side or one in front of the other.

Section 4: Tie beanbag to one end of rope. Working with partner and in space. One of the pair makes the beanbag swing around in a circle changing the rope from right hand to left hand (to prevent the child from turning around and getting dizzy) and keep beanbag just above ground (approximately 1″) while second child jumps over it. Each jump has to be different, i.e., one foot, two feet, turning in air, backwards, bunny jump over, etc. Suggest five jumps and then change partner.

FIGURE 5.41

Lesson Reminder for Lesson No. 8

CLASS ORGANIZATION

Note: At end of movement training ask class to go to section places taking ropes with them. Sections 1, 3, and 4 will be sharing ropes; knot extra ropes and leave tidily in a pile in section place.

PART I: INTRODUCTORY ACTIVITY

Either running and leaping over as many ropes as possible, or skipping on spot, or traveling.

PART II: MOVEMENT TRAINING
1. Walk along rope.
2. Jump from side to side.
3. Bridge along rope.
4. Teacher selected sequence of different ways of travel.

PART III: APPARATUS WORK
Section 1:   Different ways of skipping with partner.
Section 2:   Skipping on own with different foot patterns.
Section 3:   In twos, rope off floor, jumping pattern.
Section 4:   Beanbag knotted on to rope, one of pair swings and other jumping.

DIAGRAM G: Suggested Apparatus Arrangement for Lesson No. 8

Section 4: Beanbag on end of rope	Section 1: Partners skipping
Section 3: Skipping ropes on floor (jumping patterns)	Section 2: Skipping ropes on floor (foot patterns)

CHAPTER

SIX

Theme Three:
Understanding Direction

One of the most important aspects of movement education is the understanding and use of space. This is developed in this theme by first introducing the basic directional movements such as forward, backward, and sideways. In later lessons, emphasis is shifted to the understanding and ability to use general and personal space.

Lesson No. 1

Part I: Introductory Activity

This is a modification of an earlier lesson. Emphasis is on the use of all space, running in and out of each other in zigzag patterns. On "stop" ask them to turn half way around and then run in new direction.

FIGURE 6.1

Part II: Movement Training

When the children are in a space of their own ask them to point forward, and then by suggesting "Who can think of another direction?" one can add backward and sideways. Grade One can even manage diagonal. Continue running and jumping patterns, emphasizing change of direction after each jump.

Next, ask them to make up a sequence using forward, backward, and sideways, and a combination of running and jumping. Ask them to repeat their sequence three times and then to sit down. Select one of their ideas and have the whole class do the same sequence. For Kindergarten more assistance in sequence building will be needed than for the other grades. The inclusion of diagonal movements may be left to the following lesson if the teacher feels that four directions are too much for the class.

FIGURE 6.2

Part III: Apparatus Work

Section 1:   Find as many ways as you can get on to the box forward and off backward. (Remember to encourage rolling on landing from any apparatus.)

Section 2:   Find as many ways as you can to travel sideways along the bench and jump off the end forward. (One bench broad side up and one bench balance side up.)

FIGURE 6.3   **FIGURE 6.4**

Section 3: Each child having four beanbags arranges a pattern for himself and works out how he can go forward, backward, and sideways landing on the beanbags and not allowing his feet to touch the floor. Encourage the children to widen the space between the beanbags after each successful trial.

Section 4: Hoop vertically supported by individual mat or baseball sandbag. Choose one way of going forward either through or over hoop and a different way of traveling backward through the hoop. If no supports are available children may work in twos, one holding the hoop while the other goes through. Grades Two and Three may be able to work simultaneously, each holding hoop with one hand.

Section 5: Hoops horizontally balanced on pins. Into the hoop forward, out backward or sideways.

FIGURE 6.5

Section 6: Swinging backward and forward holding two ropes. The more adventurous will turn upside down or do "bird nests."

Section 7: Skipping backward and forward making pattern of steps either alone or with partner (twos and threes).

Section 8: Large mats. Making patterns in twos or in groups using forward, sideways, backward, and diagonal rolls. Two working from ends and two from sides as shown in Diagram H.

Lesson Reminder for Lesson No. 1

PART I: INTRODUCTORY ACTIVITY

Running, stopping, zigzag patterns with emphasis on using all space and changing directions.

PART II: MOVEMENT TRAINING

1. Pointing forward, backward, sideways, and diagonally.
2. Running, jumping, and hopping.
3. Sequence, repeat exactly three times.
4. Teacher select one sequence, teach to whole class.

PART III: APPARATUS WORK

1. Box—On forward, off backward, roll on landing.
2. Benches—Sideways along, off forward, roll on landing.
3. Beanbags—Four per child, make pattern, then travel forward, backward, sideways, using beanbags and not allowing feet to touch floor.
4. Vertical hoops supported either by mat, sandbag, or child. Travel through or over forward, and different way backward through hoop.
5. Horizontal hoops on pins. Into hoops forward, out backward or sideways.
6. Climbing ropes—Swing backward and forward between two.
7. Skipping ropes—Backward and forward pattern alone or in twos.
8. Large mats—In twos or group making pattern of all rolls.

DIAGRAM H: Suggested Apparatus Arrangement for Lessons Nos. 1, 2, 3

Section 2: Benches	Section 1: Box	Section 3: Beanbags	Section 4: 4 beanbags 2 hoops
Section 8: Large mats	Section 6: climbing ropes	Section 7: skipping ropes	Section 5: 3 pins and hoop

Lesson No. 2

Part I: Introductory Activity

"Siamese Twins." Holding partner's hand and running freely about the gymnasium. Remind the children about the use of space and to make zigzag patterns as they run over the floor. Next progress to backward, forward and sideways still holding each other.

Part II: Movement Training

Each pair in space and still holding hands. Their task is to make opposite patterns. The teacher calls out "hands"—one of the partners puts his hands

FIGURE 6.6

forward while the other puts his hands backward. Use a variety of parts and include sideways opposites and diagonal opposites. Ask them to choose three different positions and make a sequence. (Kindergarten should work alone.)

Select two pairs whose sequences differ and ask the class to comment on which directions and parts each pair uses.

Part III: Apparatus Work

Same as previous lesson.

FIGURE 6.7

Lesson Reminder for Lesson No. 2

PART I: INTRODUCTORY ACTIVITY

"Siamese twins" running and stopping—forward, backward, and sideways.

PART II: MOVEMENT TRAINING

"Siamese twins" working opposite directions for various body parts. Make up sequence of three. Get class to observe and comment.

PART III: APPARATUS WORK

1. Box—On forward, off backward.
2. Benches—Sideways along off forward.
3. Beanbags—Four per child arranged on floor. Pattern of forward, backward and sideways, traveling on to beanbags without touching floor.
4. Vertical hoops—Through or over forward and different way backward.
5. Horizontal hoops on pins (or blocks) into forward, out backward or sideways.
6. Climbing ropes—Swing forward and backward. (See Figure 6.9)
7. Skipping ropes pattern.
8. Large mats pattern.

FIGURE 6.8

FIGURE 6.9

Lesson No. 3

Part I: Introductory Activity

One beanbag for each child scattered on floor. Still stressing spacing, have the children run in and out and sometimes running around the beanbags. If they can use the space well and are controlled, then introduce a variation of speed, starting slowly and ending so that they are running very quickly. Slow down at first sign of collision and remind them about safety.

FIGURE 6.10

Part II: Movement Training

Each child working with beanbag.

"Can you make a bridge over your beanbag?"

"Now with one foot can you move your beanbag forward through one of the arches?" Practice several times.

Select one of the children who has a good example, then encourage all to try.

Choose different parts and different directions. Build a sequence of three. An example of this could be:

Position 1: Standing astride over beanbag. Bending forward, pull beanbag forward with hand without moving feet.

FIGURE 6.11

Position 2: By putting hands on floor, then using one foot to push beanbag
   sideways through arch formed by opposite leg and hand.
Position 3: Sit with legs crooked, reach with one hand and push beanbag
   sideways through arch formed by seat and feet, and catch beanbag with
   other hand.

Part III: Apparatus Work

According to the progress made and the number of turns the children
have had, keep the same apparatus but change the task.
1. Box: Use a roll along the top of the box.
2. Benches: No feet allowed on top of bench.

FIGURE 6.12   FIGURE 6.13

3. Beanbags: Toss beanbag over head with different parts.
4. Four beanbags and hoops: Transferring beanbags forward, backward or
   sideways from one hoop to another, using different parts to pick them up.
5. Horizontal hoops and pins: Jump in sideways and come out underneath
   but traveling forward.
6. Climbing ropes: If you have a row of four or more ask the children to
   travel sideways changing from one rope to next. More ambitious pupils
   can climb up at same time as change over.

FIGURE 6.14

7. Skipping ropes: Pattern of forward, backward, and sideways keeping hands and feet on floor.
8. Large mats: Change pattern to include jumping as well as rolling.

Lesson Reminder for Lesson No. 3

PART I: INTRODUCTORY ACTIVITY

Running and stopping. Beanbags scattered over floor in, out, and around with possible variation of speed.

PART II: MOVEMENT TRAINING

Beanbag for each child (if not enough beanbags, use bands, balls, or knotted skipping ropes). Bridges over beanbags using different body parts to push, pull or lift beanbag through arches. Stress moving beanbag forward, backward, or sideways. Build sequence.

PART III: APPARATUS WORK

1. Box—Use a roll to travel along top of box.
2. Benches—No feet allowed on top of bench.
3. Beanbags—Toss over head—forward and backward using different parts to pick up beanbag.
4. Four beanbags and two hoops—Using forward, backward, and sideways directions and different body parts transfer beanbag from one hoop to the other.
5. Horizontal hoops and pins—Jump in sideways and come out underneath but traveling forward.
6. Climbing ropes—Travel sideways changing from one rope to next.
7. Skipping ropes—Pattern of forward, backward, and sideways keeping hands and feet on floor.
8. Large mats—Pattern to include jumping as well as rolling.

Lesson No. 4

Part I: Introductory Activity

Scatter individual mats over gymnasium floor. Ask children to run, leap, land, and roll using either sideways safety roll or a backward diagonal roll. If no mats available this may be done freely on floor.

FIGURE 6.15

Part II: Movement Training

Make up a sequence using forward, backward, and sideways directions on mats. Remind the class that they can invent other things in addition to jumps and rolls. Select two or three sequences that show variety of activity as well as direction. Have the class comment. For example, they should be able to observe whether the child took his weight on a different body part each time he changed direction or if he chose movements that linked together to give continuity to the pattern as well as fulfilling the original task.

FIGURE 6.16

FIGURE 6.17

FIGURE 6.18

Part III: Apparatus Work

Working in subsections, that is, with no more than four to each group and each child using an individual mat (this could also be done with skipping ropes). Whisper to each group how they are to place their mats (one in a straight line, one in a circle, and one sideways or in a diagonal line). Next, ask them to invent ways of traveling along their mats in the direction they have been placed. Leave time for each group to watch others and guess the directions. Groups must be small to do this, otherwise too much time is wasted waiting a turn.

FIGURE 6.19

FIGURE 6.20

FIGURE 6.21

Lesson Reminder for Lesson No. 4

PART I: INTRODUCTORY ACTIVITY

Running, leaping, and landing and rolling using sideways and backward diagonal rolls.

PART II: MOVEMENT TRAINING

Either alone or in twos work on sequence to show different ways of moving backward, forward, sideways, and diagonally over mats.

PART III: APPARATUS WORK

In subsections work at placing mats in straight, sideways, or diagonal lines or in a circle and then invent different ways of traveling. *Must* keep groups small.

DIAGRAM I: Suggested Apparatus Arrangement for Lesson No. 4

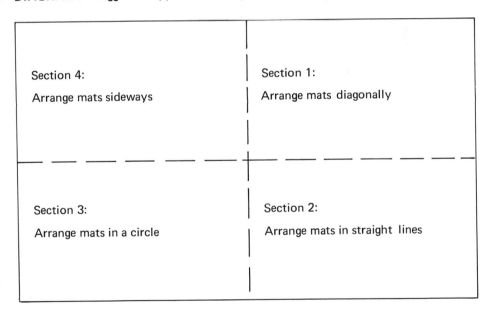

Section 4:
Arrange mats sideways

Section 1:
Arrange mats diagonally

Section 3:
Arrange mats in a circle

Section 2:
Arrange mats in straight lines

Lesson No. 5

Part I: Introductory Activity

Each child carries a hoop and runs in and out taking care to use all available space and not to collide. First Grade boys are quite good at this and will usually produce some marvelous swerving movements in order to avoid others. Change direction after each time "stop" is called.

FIGURE 6.22

Part II: Movement Training

"Can you balance the hoop on your head and step through it?"
"Can you do it sideways?"

FIGURE 6.23   **FIGURE 6.24**

"Can you do it backwards?"

"Can you balance it anywhere else and still step forward, sideways, or backward through it?"

Children in Kindergarten and Grade One will need lots of practice but thoroughly enjoy working at this. Grades Two and Three enjoy getting a partner to balance the hoop in order to climb through. Remember to stress direction by pointing out such things as "Let's watch John and Bill. Note how John is balancing the hoop on his foot. See if Bill can go through without knocking the hoop off. Which direction did Bill use to go through the hoop?"

Part III: Apparatus Work

Same as previous lesson. However, by this time you should be able to vary and add ideas to the apparatus suggested. Sometimes you will see children discover some activity in the free play time at the beginning of a lesson where they may be working on the theme from the previous lesson but have combined two types of apparatus that you had not thought of and that could easily be substituted.

Lesson Reminder for Lesson No. 5

PART I: INTRODUCTORY ACTIVITY

Running carrying a hoop. Stress spacing and change of direction.

PART II: MOVEMENT TRAINING

1. Balance hoop on head and step through.
2. Then balance on different parts.
3. Possibly working with partner.

PART III: APPARATUS WORK

Select from previous lessons.

Lesson No. 6

Part I: Introductory Activity

"Tails." Each child has a band tucked into the waist band of his shorts which makes a "tail." The aim of this activity is for the children to run using all the space and avoiding collisions and to capture as many "tails" as they can without losing their own. This game should not be played until the children have had plenty of experience in running freely in the gymnasium and can do this without any collisions. Allow sufficient time in each game for one child to capture three tails. Encourage those who have lost their "tails" to capture someone else's tail. All children should be active since there is no "being out."

FIGURE 6.25

Emphasize dodging sideways as well as backward and forward. Introduce this as being a quick and efficient way of keeping one's tail.

Part II: Movement Training

Ask each child to make a bridge shape on the floor. Find out how many arches the bridge has, that is, if both hands and feet are on the floor there

will be four arches and each arch is large enough for a partner to climb
through.

"Use your band this time and see if you can join together one foot and
one hand."

FIGURE 6.26

Try to find an example of this hole made in the following manner:
1. Behind from standing,
2. In front from standing,
3. At the side from standing,
4. Sitting down,
5. Lying down, and
6. Kneeling.

If you cannot find examples from the class ask them if they can make the
same hole or "arch" in the above ways.

"Can you join two or more different
parts together and make some new
holes? Make sure that the hole is big
enough for someone to climb through."
"Now join up in twos, one of you make
the hole while the other climbs through
without touching anything."

FIGURE 6.27

When each has had one turn ask them to make three different holes. As soon as they have climbed through, they make the hole. When they can make continuous hole or bridge sequences using a partner and a variety of apparatus, you are leading into apparatus work.

Part III: Apparatus Work

Section 1: Box: Use sides as well as top working in twos within group, make "holes" for partner to climb through.

Section 2: Wall bars or cave: Partner travels upwards, downwards, or sideways alternately making "holes" for partner to crawl through as they travel.

FIGURE 6.28   **FIGURE 6.29**

Section 3: Two climbing ropes: These may be knotted or loose, children can use these in a great variety of ways according to their ability. For example, sitting on floor holding ropes.

Section 4: Benches: Making different "holes" with part of the body on either the broad or narrow side of the bench and part on floor.

FIGURE 6.30

Section 5: Individually or in twos: Making continuous bridge over a slow rolling ball, or getting up and running after first bridge to overtake ball and then make second bridge.

Section 6: Large mats and hoop: Working in threes. Two children holding the hoop with different parts and making three or four arches. The task of the third child is to go through each arch using a different direction.

Section 7: Working individually. Hoop balanced on three pins and use all arches to crawl through.

Section 8: Two canes and two chairs: Let each child arrange own way to make maximum number of arches. Kindergarten could just work on bridges made by chairs. Grades Two and Three would work well in twos.

FIGURE 6.31   **FIGURE 6.32**

All of these activities require slow controlled movements; therefore, make sure there are other section activities such as skipping, running and jumping, climbing or swinging on ropes to provide sufficient variety of movements.

Apparatus work should always include some work from the previous lesson. The teacher can introduce one or two new ideas in each lesson when all groups have worked on the previous activities. The list of sections above shows how different apparatus can be used for this lesson plan.

Lesson 6 provides an infinite variety of movement challenges, hence the teacher can easily teach many lessons from this lesson plan, according to how quickly the members of her class think their way through the various tasks. Working with a partner will stimulate ideas and a feeling of flow can be stimulated by asking the children to climb smoothly through their holes. Movement sequences develop naturally from these activities and as with all these lesson plans, the teacher must decide whether the children have made sufficient progress in one lesson to enable them to be ready for the next, or whether the lesson should be repeated.

The children should spend at least five minutes on *each* piece of apparatus before new work is introduced. It may well be that the movement training part of the lesson may exceed ten minutes or longer in order for the children to have sufficient background to work on the apparatus. If this is the case then the second lesson should begin with the introductory activity, followed by a brief revision of the movement training and then twenty minutes spent on the apparatus, thus allowing them to cover four sections. By this stage all classes should be working in the four sections broken into subgroups. It is, therefore, possible to organize eight different apparatus activities. To cover any one of the lesson plans the teacher could spend three or more lessons developing the basic plan.

It is very important that the teacher does not present a series of new ideas which give the children a chance to explore and discover *without* giving time for repetition and refinement. Each teacher must *teach* and by this we mean clarify and expand the children's basic movement ideas. Unless some of the sequences that embody the basic ideas are developed through questions by the teacher which lead the children to a wider range and understanding, much of the potential will be lost. Further, they will not derive the satisfaction that comes with creating and working hard to produce a movement or sequence that has shape and form and can be performed at a high standard. Perhaps the best four guidelines a teacher can use to determine whether the class is ready to move on to a new lesson plan are:
1. "Have they had time to explore?"
2. "Have they had time to discover and invent?"
3. "Have they had time to repeat?"
4. "Have they reached a good standard of performance?"

Lesson Reminder for Lesson No. 6
PART I: INTRODUCTORY ACTIVITY
"Tails": Emphasize spacing, change of direction, and safety.

PART II: MOVEMENT TRAINING
Use directions of in front, behind, at side, to stimulate creativity for new ways of making "holes." Introduce levels by varying the position of "holes," standing, sitting, kneeling, lying. Vary type of "hole" by giving them choice, e.g., use band of join:
1. Both feet together,
2. Opposite hand and foot,
3. Head and foot,
4. Both hands.
Make sequence in twos continuously "holing" and crawling through. Widen their experience by suggesting that when they go through "holes" they can vary this by making different parts go first as well as by traveling forward, backward, sideways.

PART III: APPARATUS WORK

Select from the following, remembering to balance the apparatus work with vigorous whole body activities.

1. Box,
2. Wall bars, cave, or other climbing equipment,
3. Climbing ropes,
4. Benches balance or broad side up,
5. Balls,
6. Large mat and hoop working in threes,
7. Hoop on three pins,
8. Two chairs and two canes.

DIAGRAM J: Suggested Apparatus Arrangement for Lessons Nos. 6, 7, 8, 9

Section 4: Benches	Section 1: Box	Section 5: Balls	Section 2: Wall bars or CAVE
Section 3: Climbing ropes	Section 6: Large mats and hoops	Section 8: 2 chairs and canes	Section 7: Hoops and pins

Lesson No. 7

Part I: Introductory Activity

So far we have not had any plan dealing specifically with levels. For primary grades, the easiest way to introduce this is by contrasting high and low movements. Ask children to run holding partner's hand. On "stop," one partner makes herself as small and low to the ground as possible while the other makes herself as high as possible. Kindergarten and Grade One love to play Jack-in-the-Box, hence, for them instead of saying "stop" use "Jack-in-the-Box," and they will quickly shoot up high or quickly drop down.

FIGURE 6.33

As soon as they have understood and have the feel of being high or low, isolate different parts of the body, i.e., one finger, feet, and then let each pair choose which part they will make high or low.

Part II: Movement Training

Keeping the same partner in Grades Two and Three, let them invent three "highs and lows," using different parts of their bodies and remaining in contact with their partners.

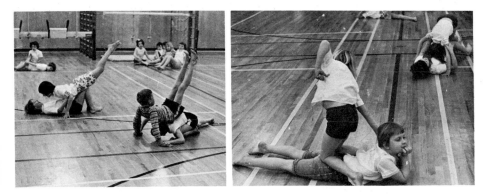

FIGURE 6.34   **FIGURE 6.35**

Part III: Apparatus Work

Apply partner work to apparatus.

1. Box: Each pair making sequence on top of box. Grades Two and Three may like to work up from floor as side of box can often be used as a support for them.
2. Benches: Invent a high-low sequence traveling along the bench.
3. Climbing ropes: Sequence of two movements so that each partner has turn at being low and high.

4. Climbing equipment or climbing ropes: "Go as high as you can and then climb down." Allow lots of turns. Do not make this competitive— work individually.
5. Hoops:) Working alone or with partner to make sequence of picking up
6. Balls:) Balls or hoops with different parts, taking them as high as possible and then putting them down and picking up again with a different part. Remember to add forward, backward, and sideways to high and low for variety and added range.

FIGURE 6.36   FIGURE 6.37

7. Beanbags: Using different parts to toss beanbags into the air and then pick up with different parts, i.e., "shaggy dog," "bunny jump," with beanbag between feet, etc.
8. Stage and large mats: Jumping as high as they can, landing and rolling.
9. Benches tied to ropes: Running and leaping high, landing and rolling.
10. Canes and chairs: Leaping over to get high, rolling under to keep low.

FIGURE 6.38   FIGURE 6.39

Lesson Reminder for Lesson No. 7

PART I: INTRODUCTORY ACTIVITY

"Siamese twins," running, stopping—Jack-in-the-Box whole body, then different parts and final time let each pair decide on own.

PART II: MOVEMENT TRAINING

In pairs, work at contrasting high and low with different parts. Make sequence of three different highs and lows. Make sure that each child has turn of both high and low positions.

PART III: APPARATUS WORK

Select from:

1. Box—Using top and sides.
2. Benches—Traveling along.
3. Climbing ropes—Two positions.
4. Climbing equipment or ropes—"Climb as high as you can." *Individual* not competitive.
5. & 6. Hoops—Balls—With partner or alone pick up with different parts lifting high, add forward, backward, sideways to extend range.
7. Beanbags—Tossing for height.
8. Stage and Mats—High leap, land and roll.
9. Benches and climbing ropes—High leap, land and roll.
10. Chairs and canes—Leap over and roll under.

Lesson No. 8

Part I: Introductory Activity

If you have four or more benches, have the children space them on the floor anywhere in the gymnasium but away from the walls. This activity should only be attempted after the initial period of safety training has taken place. Do not teach this in your first month of Movement Education. Ask the children to run and leap over or step up and leap into the air, then land and roll without colliding and using all available space.

FIGURE 6.40   **FIGURE 6.41**

Part II: Movement Training

Working individually, using a beanbag and finding a space on one of the benches, practice jumping off bench over beanbag placed on floor, and landing with a safety roll. Encourage the placing of the beanbag farther away from the bench each time they leap over and also vary the high jumps by asking them to leap high forward, backward, or sideways always landing with a safety roll. Also stress that they try to find different ways and directions of returning to the bench.

FIGURE 6.42

Part III: Apparatus Work

Select from Lesson 7.

Lesson Reminder for Lesson No. 8

PART I: INTRODUCTORY ACTIVITY

Benches placed freely on floor away from walls. Leaping on to and off or over benches landing with roll, watching spacing.

PART II: MOVEMENT TRAINING

Working individually with beanbag in a space on the bench. Leaping over beanbag on floor and rolling on landing. Increase difficulty by moving position of beanbag, jumping in different directions returning to bench in different way.

PART III: APPARATUS WORK

Select from Lesson 7.

Lesson No. 9

Part I: Introductory Activity

By using a slight variation of Jack-in-the-Box and using the words "up and down" instead of "high and low," the basis is laid for the rest of this lesson.

FIGURE 6.43   FIGURE 6.44

Part II: Movement Training

Working individually curled up small in a space. Make fingers lead the movement, gradually reach up until fingers are stretched and the child is standing on tiptoes. When he cannot reach up any higher, he comes down and curls up in a ball as quickly as possible. Practice several turns.

"Now can you stay down and take up a lot of room on the floor? Are your tummies, legs, head, and arms all touching the floor? This time make yourself thinner and thinner until you are long and thin and straight. Make your wide shape on the floor again. Now make your narrow shape where you are long and thin. Let me see you doing this standing up."

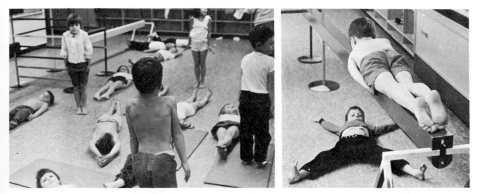

FIGURE 6.45   FIGURE 6.46

Experiment with different wide and narrow shapes taking weight on different parts of the body. "Can you invent a jump that goes backward and forward?"

Practice different parts leading in the up and down and experiment with various ways of being wide and narrow, and backward and forward. The teacher can select shapes to form a sequence and then have the whole class try to join them together. Finally add "quick and slow" to provide a contrast in time as well as space.

Part III: Apparatus Work

Select from:

1. Box   )   "Jump down off the apparatus and make
2. Benches   )   either a wide shape or a narrow shape
3. Stage   )   in the air."
4. Ropes and benches)
5. Two climbing ropes   )   Two wide shapes and two narrow shapes working
6. Wall bars or climbing)   sideways or upside down as well as right side up
   equipment   )   and using different body parts to support weight.

FIGURE 6.47

FIGURE 6.48

Lesson Reminder for Lesson No. 9

PART I: INTRODUCTORY ACTIVITY

"Jack-in-the-Box" running using up and down as directions.

PART II: MOVEMENT TRAINING

Working individually in a space, curled up small, fingers (or other part) leading stretching up, quickly down back into ball.

Begin with wide and narrow, then progress to different parts taking weight.

Invent jump that goes backward and forward. Make class sequence and add quick and slow.

PART III: APPARATUS WORK

Jump down off apparatus making either wide shape or narrow shape in air.
1. Box.
2. Benches.
3. Stage.
4. Ropes and benches.

Make two wide shapes and two narrow shapes (extend their range by inviting them to work sideways or upside down as well as right side up and by taking weight off different body parts).
5. Two climbing ropes.
6. Wall bars or other climbing equipment.

SEVEN

Theme Four: Qualities

It is impossible to teach in the gymnasium or on the playground without using combinations of time, space, force, and flow. Up to this point we have taken space as our main theme and have explored it in many ways. We have used large and small spaces and emphasized how different body parts can use this space, and we have used the space in front, behind, and at the side. By including jumping activities from the ground or off apparatus, different levels of space have been introduced. For all of these activities we are unconsciously using time, force and flow. At this stage we feel that to enable the children's movement knowledge and imagination to continue to grow we should now develop their conscious understanding and appreciation of time, force, and flow. This is like a chef adding his seasoning which, in turn, becomes an integral and inseparable part of his gourmet dish. So too, the children learn to select and emphasize various qualities which are already a part of their movement sequences in order to produce a satisfying and complete work. It is also important for the children not to isolate the qualities. Perhaps the latter can best be illustrated by a small girl who, having played her piano piece with exactly the right notes and in strict time, turned to her teacher and asked "Now shall I play it with expression?"

FIGURE 7.1

How then do we set about bringing out these various qualities? One of the most effective ways we have found with primary children is through the dance approach. The majority of teachers find it easier to work toward a freer approach in the gymnasium through gymnastics. We have not included dance in this Introduction to Movement Education; however, ideally dance gymnastics and games should go hand in hand since each enhances the other. This next lesson plan has worked in an endless number of situations where children have had no previous experience in any form of Movement Education. In this lesson plan, time, space, force, and flow are all explored, developed, and linked together by focusing the child's attention on the antics of a ten cent balloon.

Lesson No.1 (Time, Space, Force, and Flow)

Part I: Introductory Activity

The children should be sitting in the middle of the gymnasium with the teacher in the middle of the group.

"Children, I have a secret in my hand. If I give you a clue, do you think you can guess what it is? If I blow into it, it will get bigger" (be prepared for the one who suggests bubble-gum!). "That's right, my secret is a balloon! Now, look how tiny the balloon is; it is hardly taking up any space at all, but when I blow into it, it will get bigger and take up more room. Now, you are sitting in the middle of the gymnasium and taking up very little space. Look at all the space we have left in the gymnasium. As I blow into the balloon and make it take up more space, you must move into a bigger space. There is just one rule, you can only move when I am blowing into the balloon, so you must always keep your eyes on the balloon."

When the balloon is fairly large, ask the children what they think they should do now, and begin to let the air out of the balloon. They will instinctively start moving back to the center. This is an opportunity to emphasize spacing. As they come back they must move carefully and not bump into anyone.

The second time let the air out slowly and ask them to move slowly back (introducing time). Repeat two or three times according to how well they used the space. The last time, when they are well spaced, have them gradually get smaller on the spot until they are very tiny and curled up in a ball. Allow two or three turns at getting as big and taking up as much room as they can in their own space.

Next, let them watch you tie the balloon into a knot (when it is blown up!) and ask them to tie themselves into a knot. Do not keep them in this position for too long. Look at some of the different types of knots so that when they "burst," you could use one or two as demonstrations. Let them "burst" so they are flat on the floor (this makes speed and causes wide shapes to form). The second time ask them to tie a much more complicated knot and to start in the standing position twisting slowly to tie a very tight, hard knot. When all are tied ask them if they can make it tighter still, then have them bursting and stress the quick sudden movement to make a wide shape on the floor (as a contrast to the small tight knot). Repeat as necessary, and select children who have good knots or quick bursts.

Toss the balloon into the air and let it float down. Ask them if they know the word that describes how the balloon comes down. Even at the Grade One level there is always one child who says "floating." Invite them to float their fingers down as gently as the balloon floats down. Make sure they watch their own fingers (usually they find this quite difficult).

FIGURE 7.2

FIGURE 7.3

For contrast, punch the balloon into the air and again ask them for the word that describes the action. Make sure that before you invite them to try this each child is in his own space and understands that he is to punch as hard as he can upwards into the air. The direction is important for there is the risk that the boys may try a few right hooks on each other. Dissipate their energies by strong hard punching *upwards* or *downwards*.

Another safety precaution is to let them shout "punch" as they do it, but have them ready to punch at the same time; otherwise it is difficult to make oneself heard as they usually do this with great vigor and enthusiasm! (Allow only one shout at each punch.) When they gather themselves to punch ask them to make a tight fist so that they can punch hard; emphasize the quick explosive movement and the strength and force necessary to perform this.

FIGURE 7.4

If you think that they are ready you can now suggest that they imagine how the balloon would travel if the string snapped and it was blown by the wind. To begin with they will probably just "whosh" around the room without making much of a pattern. Tell them you want to see whether the wind is having fun and playing tricks on the balloon, sometimes leaving it quite still and not blowing it at all, other times blowing it up into the air, and others where the wind is blowing so hard the balloon has to go very fast.

Finally ask them what usually happens to a balloon if it gets blown into a tree, and the usual reply will be "pop."

"Pop" the balloon and ask the children to watch what happens to the pieces—"Do they drop straight to the ground, or do they go upwards first and then drop, or what do they do?" Then let them try "popping" themselves. Again you can get the children to provide the sound effects! (quick explosive movement).

FIGURE 7.5

This lesson will take at least thirty to forty minutes if the children are to get anything from it, hence, you may like to try part of the lesson in one period, ending up with the wind blowing the balloon, and the rest in a second period. Again repeat the wind blowing part of the lesson, but expect them to be able to repeat exactly what their balloon does this time.

Questions That May Assist:
1. From which spot on the gymnasium floor do they start?
2. Are they standing or sitting or are they curled up in a ball?
3. Is the wind gentle or strong to start with?
4. What sort of tricks does the wind play on them?

In the lesson reminder there are questions which give some leads as to what you may like to stress and also to help you observe what the children can do in a lesson of this type. From this you should also be able to gather some ideas regarding your class's needs. You may find, for instance, that their spacing is good, (it ought to be by this stage as a result of the emphasis on this during safety training), but they may not be very good at quick and slow movements. Young children find it hard to maintain a speed which is not natural to them so during the next few lessons you might provide opportunities for responding with very quick movements and very slow ones. The latter leads into the next lesson.

Lesson Reminder for Lesson No. 1

BALLOONS

1. Look to see how the children space themselves from the central group.
   Do they scatter evenly?
   Do they improve when activity is repeated?

2. When returning to the center—
   Do they rush back in uncontrolled manner pushing each other as they go?
   Are they interested in controlling their movements to keep in time with the balloon?

3. When making themselves as large as they can in their own space—
   Do they reach up with hands together above their heads?
   Do they spread themselves, hands and feet wide apart?

4. When making themselves as small as they can—
   Do they tuck in as much as they can?
   Do they lie flat on the floor?
   Do they crouch on tiptoes with everything tucked in?

5. When tying themselves in a knot—
   Do they tie arms and legs separately?
   Do they intertwine arms and legs?
   Do they twist rather than bend their bodies?

6. When they "burst"—
   Do they jump up as they "burst"?
   Do they lie down?
   Is it a quick movement?

7. When they "float" their hands down—
   Do they watch their fingers?
   Is there any feeling in the quality of their movement?
   Do they find it easy?

8. When they punch—
   Are they strong and firm?
   Can they hold the position?
   Does the quality of their movement improve when they say the word as they punch?

9. When asked to punch in different directions—
   Do they, or do they not use the same arm?

10. When they are moving around the room—
    Do they stay on one level?
    Do they leap in the air?
    Do they sink to the ground?
    Do they swirl around?

Lesson No. 2 (Time)

Part I: Introductory Activity

Running in the gymnasium taking very short and quick steps and alternating with long slow giant strides. Small quick step running is more fun when changing direction and long slow giant strides when traveling in a straight line. (Figure 7.13)

Part II: Movement Training

Sitting in a group in the middle of the gymnasium tapping hands on the floor, starting slowly and getting faster, then slowing down again. Several

FIGURE 7.6

FIGURE 7.7

FIGURE 7.8

turns, then do the same with the feet. Now moving slowly, gently and care-fully (not bumping into anyone), find a space. Then lie on backs with legs in the air and shake their feet as hard and as fast as they can. Then up on their feet again traveling slowly until they find a new space. This time, down on their backs and quick shaking of feet. Now can they find a different way of traveling slowly without using their feet? When they find another space can they move a different part very quickly?

Part III: Apparatus Work

You can draw on any previous lessons and will find, as stated earlier, that certain activities lend themselves easily to stressing quality and thus making the movement more complete. For example, any balance work is more effec-tive if slow and controlled—so benches for balance work could be one section. Balancing of balls, beanbags or hoops and traveling also would require slow smooth movements and could be another section.

| FIGURE 7.9 | FIGURE 7.10 | FIGURE 7.11 |

For quick movements skipping is ideal, and any form of jumping off apparatus lends itself to quick explosive movements requiring leg strength. Also making up quick foot patterns in and out of, or around beanbags and hoops, and skipping ropes can be fun. Rolling on mats as fast as possible or any apparatus activity produces lots of interesting sequences.

Grade Three children are capable of making excellent sequences of roll-ing which show contrast of speeds.

FIGURE 7.12

Lesson Reminder for Lesson No. 2

PART I: INTRODUCTORY ACTIVITY

Running with quick small steps making zigzag floor patterns and long slow giant strides on straight lines.

PART II: MOVEMENT TRAINING

Hands tapping floor, feet tapping floor, moving slowly to space, quick feet in air, change moving to a new space slowly without using feet, then moving different part very quickly.

PART III: APPARATUS WORK

Select from previous work where quick and slow could be applied.

Lesson No. 3 (Strength and Lightness)

Part I: Introductory Activity

The teacher should now be particularly concerned with developing an understanding of how to apply force in order to gain height. Movement challenges should emphasize a strong push with the legs, straightening at hip, knee, and ankle joints, and getting the final "maximum" lift with the push off from the toes. By this stage, children should not have any problems in running freely without collisions, hence, other points may be stressed such as lifting head and arms to help the lift. Younger children tend to try to jump high by looking at their toes. To counteract this, encourage short periods of "star gazing" as they leap.

Part II: Movement Training

A quick revision of "shooting feet" as this mobility in the ankle joint and toes is important to apply the force and strength necessary for jumping.

Jumping while a partner sits and looks to see if his partner's knees are straight and feet stretched with toes pointed. Children should now be able to watch each other—even Grade One. Assist them to understand the need for explosive force, for example, by suggesting they shoot into the air like a rocket. Also re-emphasize that they try to land lightly even though they straightened their hips, knees, ankles and toes in order to jump upwards, they must bend everything as they come down to prevent landing with a bump.

FIGURE 7.13

Part III: Apparatus Work

1. Benches: Running along to gather speed, jump up, land, and roll.
2. Benches: Pulling themselves along top of bench to develop arm strength. (See Figure 7.15)
3. Box: Leaping on to box, getting off by taking weight on arms (this can be done in a variety of ways).
4. Rope climbing: Using arms only for climbing up.
5. Climbing equipment: Any activity where weight is taken by the arms. (See Figure 7.16)
6. Hoop held by partner: Leaping into hoop and bunny jump out so that weight is taken on arms.
7. Using gymnasium walls: Lying face downward on floor with feet against wall, pushing up on arms and walk feet up wall. This can also be done with beanbags on edge of platform so that once their feet are as high as the platform they can knock beanbags on to the floor with their feet. (See Figure 7.17)

FIGURE 7.14

FIGURE 7.15

FIGURE 7.16

8. One lying on back and using his feet to balance his partner. Starts by child A lying on back, legs bent with feet in air. Child B takes hold of child A's hands and leans with his tummy against A's feet. "A" straightens his legs slowly thus taking B's weight and tries to balance B in the air.

FIGURE 7.17

Lesson Reminder for Lesson No. 3

PART I: INTRODUCTORY ACTIVITY

Running, leaping, and landing. Stress straightening leg joints, push with toes, head and arms upwards, to help flight.

PART II: MOVEMENT TRAINING

Revise "shooting feet" for mobility and strength.

Working in twos, one jumping while other observes and coaches. Stress also light landings.

PART III: APPARATUS WORK

1. Benches—Running, leaping, landing, and rolling.
2. Benches—Arm strength—pulling themselves along broad side of bench.
3. Box—Jumping on to and off with weight on arms.
4. Rope climbing.
5. Climbing equipment—Any activity where weight is taken by arms either right side up or upside down.
6. Hoops—Held by partner, leap in, bunny jump out.
7. Walk up gymnasium wall or platform. Use beanbags as target if possible.
8. Lying on back taking partner's weight with feet.

Lesson No. 4 (Combining Time and Flow)

Part I: Introductory Activity

Running quickly in zigzag patterns, freezing into a pose on "stop." Each time freeze into different pose.

FIGURE 7.18

Part II: Movement Training

While holding partner's hands in a crossed position, twirling and freezing into statues. The teacher should direct the amount of "twirling" time to prevent the children from going on too long and becoming giddy. This is where "flow" can be emphasized, with the smooth continuous twirling followed by a jerky "stop." A greater variety of statues can be stimulated if the teacher varies height and stresses different body parts. For example, "Freeze this time with one elbow on the ground" or "One have knees high and the other knees low down." Remember, the main emphasis is on the smooth continuous twirl and the sudden stop.

FIGURE 7.19   **FIGURE 7.20**

Part III: Apparatus Work

Use any available large or small apparatus. Each child should be working individually (or with a partner) traveling around, over, on any piece of apparatus, keeping the flow of movement continuous until the "stop" signals each child to freeze into a statue. Encourage many angular or spiky shapes for the statues, then let them slowly "melt" into smooth traveling again. Make sure that all movements on and off are as fluent as possible to contrast with the "freezing" of the statues.

FIGURE 7.21

Lesson Reminder for Lesson No. 4

PART I: INTRODUCTORY ACTIVITY

Running, stopping, and freezing into statues.

PART II: MOVEMENT TRAINING

Statues in twos. Twirling and freezing into many shapes. Stress continuous twirl, jerky freeze. Use different levels and body parts to produce variety.

PART III: APPARATUS WORK

All available climbing, agility, and small apparatus. Flowing smoothly anywhere in the gymnasium and "freezing" into statues wherever they are on "stop."

Lesson No. 5 (Flow)

Part I: Introductory Activity

Use the apparatus part of the previous lesson where all apparatus is out and children move around over, across, or through until "stop" is called, signaling them to freeze into statues.

Part II: Movement Training

On the basis of the previous lesson, ask them to select their three best statues and, using a partner, join them together. Start in a "freeze" position with first pose, melt gradually and move continuously until ready to "freeze" into second statue and same to the third statue. The teacher now selects different statues from each of three pairs (or if one pair produces a sufficiently varied sequence use that) and have the whole class learn and perform this new sequence. This is particularly good for observation of movement by children as well as training their movement memories.

FIGURE 7.22   **FIGURE 7.23**

Part III: Apparatus Work

Work in groups with Grades Two and Three and using any type of apparatus work out a group sequence. All *must* be on apparatus or somehow in contact with it at all times. Still keep to three statues and again stress movement memory and observation.

Broom handles, large bamboo canes, skipping ropes, hoops, as well as benches, box, platform, and climbing apparatus are all excellent for this type of activity.

FIGURE 7.24   FIGURE 7.25   FIGURE 7.26

Lesson Reminder for Lesson No. 5

PART I: INTRODUCTORY ACTIVITY

Freely moving and "freezing" a variety of apparatus. Encourage imaginative statues.

FIGURE 7.27

PART II: MOVEMENT TRAINING

In twos, three statues "melting" and "freezing" into sequence. Develop class sequence.

PART III: APPARATUS WORK

For Grades Two and Three, group sequence keeping in contact with apparatus all the time.
1. Broom handles or bamboo canes.
2. Skipping ropes.
3. Hoops.
4. Benches.
5. Box.
6. Climbing equipment.

DIAGRAM K: Suggested Apparatus Arrangement for Lesson Nos. 5, 6

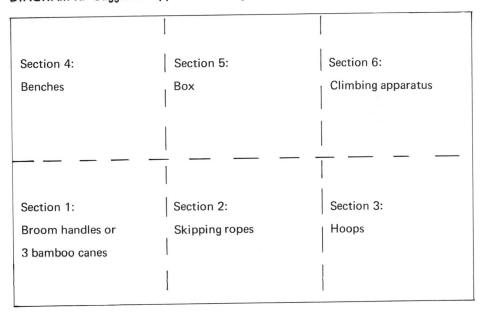

Lesson No. 6 (Flow and Speed)

As already discussed in Lesson 1, direction can and does combine with flow and speed. As the children's knowledge and understanding of movement increases so does their movement imagination and creativity. It is worthwhile going back over some of the earlier lesson plans, and using ideas covered there, show how the work they have done since the earlier lesson enables them to find different ways of exploring the same ideas. For instance, by combining different parts high with wide and narrow to form sequences instead of the rather stilted and isolated movements that evolved some lessons earlier, it should now be possible for them not only to invent new solutions but to vary the speed and flow of their sequence. As their earlier attempts usually consist of jerky movements, flow would now be stressed along with a change from one shape to another.

FIGURE 7.28

Part I: Introductory Activity

One of the easiest ways to introduce shape is by using letters of the alphabet.

Running and stopping, with either the teacher selecting the letter they should form on "stop" or allowing the children to select their own. Grade Three usually do this very well working with a partner, thus making it possible to form a greater variety of letters.

Part II: Movement Training

"X's", "V's", and "Y's" make useful wide shapes. Invite the children to make them standing as well as lying down. Many in Grades Two and Three and often in Kindergarten and Grade One are able to do handstands, headstands, cartwheels, and change from wide to narrow shapes in the process. Once they have decided on what narrow and wide shapes they wish to use in their sequence the emphasis then becomes on *how* they move from one to the other. Decisions must be made as to the order. Often for Grade One and Kindergarten, a good guideline is to ask them to choose one shape where they are lying down, one sitting, and the third one standing. Older children make much more interesting patterns if allowed to decide on their own. Again phrases that will help produce variety are "Twist from your first wide shape to your second" or "Roll into your third shape."

Permit the children to try out their own ideas first and observe any children who develop interesting ways of getting from one to the next shape.

Part III: Apparatus Work

All groups working at moving from one wide shape to another either individually or as a group. Remember *how* they go from one to the other is important but the actual quality of their shape is also very important. For example, are toes pointed if legs are supposed to be stretched? They must "feel" the movement the whole way through their bodies and know what each part of them is doing.

FIGURE 7.29

Lesson Reminder for Lesson No. 6

PART I: INTRODUCTORY ACTIVITY

Running and stopping alphabet letters for wide and narrow shapes.

PART II: MOVEMENT TRAINING

Making wide shapes from different starting positions, that is, from standing or sitting. Concentrate on *how* they move from one to the other as well as the quality of the actual shape. After allowing time for them to select their own shapes and methods of changing from one to the other, extend the challenge by asking them to "twist from the first to the second shape," and to "roll from the second to the third position."

PART III: APPARATUS WORK

All groups working at moving from one wide shape to another on the apparatus either alone or as a group.

1. Benches.
2. Box.
3. Climbing equipment.
4. Hoops.
5. Canes.
6. Skipping rope.

FIGURE 7.30   **FIGURE 7.31**   **FIGURE 7.32**

Teaching Points

1. In each lesson there should be opportunities for the children to explore, select, refine, and repeat. The balance is left to the teacher to decide by observing the needs of her class.
2. Observation is the key feature of the capable teacher of Movement Education. It is through observation that she will be able to decide upon the needs of her class.
3. From this observation the teacher will have discovered many new movement patterns and ways of using apparatus and thus will have this experience to help her teach her next class. Even though you are busy with a hundred-and-one things to do, jot down ideas that the children invent. Although you may feel certain that you will not forget by next year, many of those ideas will have faded from your mind. Some classes are more imaginative than others and you will be more confident with the knowledge that the activities invented by previous classes are suitable for children of that grade level.
4. We have tried to use a variety of apparatus in the lesson plans. We also realize that many teachers will have little equipment to work with at this stage. However, it is possible to work on many movement ideas with little or no apparatus and we included the ten cent balloon lesson to demonstrate this.

One primary teacher who herself has no formal training at all in this method and no equipment has taught valuable movement lessons to children by using a Grade One science lesson where they watched water boil and then followed the freezing process by continual peeps into the refrigerator. This was immediately followed up by movement experiences in the activity room, and what fun the children had! Another lesson on the life cycle of a butterfly proved interesting to children of Grade One with the boys pretending to be caterpillars while the girls enjoyed the butterfly part of the lesson. They both delighted in the "grub" and the "larvae" stages.

If you are adventurous enough to try teaching with this method, be adventurous enough to try out your own ideas and only fall back on this book as a "prop." Improvise, capitalize, and observe, and both you and the children will enjoy the lesson.

One final word, many parts of the lesson plans for the intermediate grades will be fun for the primary grades, so don't be afraid to turn the page.

PART THREE

A Movement Education
Program
for Intermediate Grades

Chapter 8. Theme One: Safety Training
Chapter 9. Theme Two: Adding to the Range and Understanding of Movement
Chapter 10. Theme Three: Stretching and Curling
Chapter 11. Theme Four: Change of Direction
Chapter 12. Theme Five: Twisting

Part Three represents a full year's program for Grades Four through Seven. Since the majority of teachers using this book will be embarking upon their first attempt to use the Movement Education approach, numerous lesson plans have been described in detail. Any lesson included within each of the five suggested themes may be, with slight variations, taught to any class in the intermediate grades. The rationale underlying this statement is logical and valid. In this approach to teaching physical education, children of various ages may be given the same task and apparatus and even the same layout of apparatus. However, since each child is allowed to respond to each movement task according to his own level of physical ability and creative imagination, sufficient scope and challenge are inherent in any lesson. Further, progression of skill and movement ideas becomes an individualized matter, hence no arbitrary standard of performance can be demanded according to grade level or any other normative standard.

The first two or three lessons of each theme are described and illustrated in some detail. Each succeeding lesson is much briefer simply because one builds upon each preceding lesson.

Within each theme there are "Lesson Reminders." Once you are reasonably familiar with a lesson, use the "Lesson Reminder" in the gymnasium as a "quick" reference to movement tasks and general layout of apparatus.

Since the Movement Education approach to learning may be simultaneously introduced to the primary grades, Part Two is arranged in the same format as the intermediate grades. Intermediate teachers should review Part Two to understand the similarities in approach and the differences in performance expected of younger children.

EIGHT

Theme One:
Safety Training

The underlying principles and importance of safety training have been discussed in Part One and illustrated in Part Two. In this chapter, the same emphasis will be given with a change only in the approach. The latter considers the characteristics of this age group, their previous physical education experiences, and other related factors.

As previously stated, the atmosphere of a physical education lesson which is approached in this way must be the same as any informal and relaxed classroom setting. Initially, teachers may find this atmosphere hard to achieve, particularly where children have been used to traditional teaching methods and where formal discipline was emphasized.

Removal of rigid control may temporarily result in undisciplined behaviour. A conflict may exist between the child's feeling of compulsion to work under the threat of punishment and the feeling of freedom to do as he wishes in a less structured situation.

One of the great advantages of this method is that children have an opportunity to learn self-discipline.

In the initial lessons there is a need to teach the important safety training principles and, at the same time, begin to develop an informal teaching atmosphere. Both factors are considered in the accompanying introductory lessons. One of the first things to learn is to run freely in and out of each other without bumping and without talking or making excessive noise. The children must learn to listen for your voice since you no longer use a whistle, and must learn to break the habit of always running in a circle formation around the gymnasium. These two factors may appear to be insignificant; however, they are the key to the beginning of a successful movement education program. When children have learned to move freely and quietly in multiple directions without bumping, they are ready for this approach.

The following "beginning" activities will assist each teacher in achieving this atmosphere. These activities are primarily designed to capture the children's interest and to force them into working quietly in order to hear your voice.

How to Begin

As the children come into the gymnasium it is important to give them something to do right away, and to keep each child busy for the entire lesson. Hence, the first few children to enter the gymnasium should get out the apparatus and arrange it at the sides of the gymnasium so that it will be ready for the last half of the lesson. As other children arrive, allow them to practice ball skills, handstands, or other stunts, until all the children are in the gymnasium. In subsequent lessons, this time can be used to practice something from previous lessons. When everyone is changed and in the gymnasium, tell them to stop what they are doing and come to you (asking them to sit on the floor around you) in order to hear what you have to say. You should emphasize that you have no whistle, hence, when they run it will have to be very quietly or else they will not be able to hear you. One should also explain to the children the value of this approach, from their point of view and from yours. Experienced teachers know that when children are treated as intelligent human beings, they, in turn, will show sensitivity and enthusiasm toward new ideas.

Lesson No. 1

For your first lesson, scatter enough hoops for each child at random over the floor. (An alternate first introductory activity is provided later for those who do not have enough hoops.)

Part I: Introductory Activity

Tell the children that they are to run in and out of the hoops without touching either a hoop or each other. Stress "no talking" and "feet light" so they can hear you say "change." As soon as you call "change," each child jumps quickly into the nearest hoop.

"Are you ready? Off you go!"

If there is too much noise, clap your hands and verbally reinforce your point, that is, insist on less noise so that you and the children can get on with the activity.

"Change!" and everybody should quickly jump into a hoop.

During this activity did you learn anything about your class? For example, did they run quickly, boldly weaving in and out? Did they constantly run around the outside of the room? Did they really use their feet properly

FIGURE 8.1

as they ran? Did they push or giggle? All these things will be discussed, bit by bit, during the course of the next few lessons.

Now take one hoop away and, on the same principle of musical chairs, explain that the next time you say "change," one person will be without a hoop. The "last" child may, if you like, do some simple thing chosen by the class (make a funny face or do an exercise a number of times), or you may take the opportunity to learn the child's name if he is new to the class. Repeat this activity four or five times, varying the amount of time you keep them moving and always stressing the following points:

1. Moving quietly,
2. Weaving in and out of the hoops using an interesting floor pattern, that is, *not* just running around one hoop or running solely around the outside of the gymnasium, and
3. running as quickly as is possible while maintaining control.

An Alternate Introductory Activity

Ask the class to run anywhere in the gymnasium and when you say "stop," everyone must freeze to the spot. Re-emphasize the fact that you have no whistle so only those with sharp ears and quiet feet will hear you, particularly as you are not going to raise your voice.

"Let's see who can be the first person to stop. Off you go . . . "stop."

"That was good." (Hopefully)

"Next time I am going to call out a direction instead of "stop" and you must keep running in that direction until I call out the next one or tell you to stop."

Almost as soon as they have started, call out "backward," then "forward," "backward," "sideways," etc. Vary the timing and give them a good run before they rest. Tell the class what you expect of them, such as a quick response, quiet feet, and careful use of space when changing direction in order not to bump into anyone.

This part of the lesson should take about five minutes, and should set the theme and the "tone" of your lesson. Following this, tell the class to find a good space for themselves, anywhere in the gymnasium and *not* too close to anyone or the wall, then sit down facing you. You are ready for the second part of the lesson, Movement Training.

Part II: Movement Training

Explain to the children that during the next few lessons they will be learning to "roll" out of a fall or from various landing positions. Emphasize there are many different kinds of rolls and that they will *all* eventually be able to do them. Stress that one, the sideways safety roll, will help to protect them when they begin to work at the large apparatus.

One of the first and easiest rolls is the backward diagonal roll.

If there are small mats (individual) available, use them. If not, use all available large mats or the floor (see Simon Fraser University's Film 1 described in Appendix A). The following progression will help in teaching the backward diagonal roll.

1. Clasp your arms around your knees (knees should be bent up to the chest).
2. Now simply "round out" the base of your spine, rock backward and forward and sit up.

FIGURE 8.2

FIGURE 8.3

3. Allow children to practice this several times and find a child who is able to do it smoothly and easily. Get him to demonstrate. If the children get the feeling of "melting" into the floor, they will not hurt their backs.
4. Next, unclasp your knees and use your hands to help you to get *both* knees over *one* shoulder. Quickly find a child to demonstrate. Allow time for additional practice.

5. Next, increase the momentum of your rocking and try to go right over taking the weight on to your feet. Put your thumbs near your ears and you will find that your hands are in the right position to help push you over.

FIGURE 8.4

This movement is not painful on the hard floor as no weight is taken on the head. Within a lesson or two *all* the children will be able to do this roll. Furthermore, it will give those who have always found "rolls" difficult an immediate sense of achievement.

6. If the class is progressing well, move on to combining a backward diagonal roll with a small jump on the spot. Make sure each child lands with a complete bending of the knees in order to move smoothly into the roll.

Teaching Points
1. Allow the children to have several turns, practicing on their own while you watch carefully.
2. After getting two or three children to demonstrate, let them all practice again while the visual image is fresh.
3. "Rounding" the back and controlling the "rock" is essential.

This part of the lesson normally lasts about ten minutes; however, for your first lesson reduce the time to approximately five to six minutes.

Part III: Apparatus Work

Immediately after the Movement Training part of the lesson choose six team leaders (for a class of 30-36 children) then place the remaining children on each of the teams. Use your own method of arranging teams. All teams now listen carefully while you tell them what each will do and where they will do it. Your instructions might allow children to arrange equipment according to diagram shown under Lesson Reminder at the end of this lesson.

1. *First team: Two mats*

Combine any rolls you know including the backward diagonal roll. At least two people should use the mat at the same time.

FIGURE 8.5

OR

1. *First team: Two benches and wall bars*

Incline two benches on the wall bars (or Southampton Cave) by their hooks at about shoulder height (improvise where necessary). Climb up to the top of the bench by the bars and think of three different ways of coming down the bench. Move as quickly as you can to avoid line-ups. Roll on to the floor as you leave the bench.

FIGURE 8.6   **FIGURE 8.7**   **FIGURE 8.8**

2. *Second team: Three or four benches and mat*

    Benches to be arranged as for "storming," that is, running up an inclined bench, leaping off and landing with a roll on a mat.

    The benches are arranged in the following manner: First bench broadside up, second bench narrow side up on top of first one, and third bench inclined by hooks on to the narrow side of the second bench (see Simon Fraser University's Films 1 and 5).

    Two children should sit (taking turns) at either end of the benches to stabilize them. After running up the bench and jumping, landing and rolling, some children may like to turn in the air in order to practice the backward diagonal roll. A feeling of flight should be encouraged by a strong push from the bench to get height into the air, after they have learned to control their landing and roll on the mat.

3. *Third team: Vaulting box less two layers and two mats.* (Cafeteria benches can be used in lieu of a vaulting box.)

    Arrange mats at each end and slightly to the side of the box. This group divides into two and stands at either end. Run at the same time as your partner, (who is approaching from the opposite direction), pass him on the top of the box without touching, leap off and roll on mat. Later, children will think of a different way of passing their partner on the box.

FIGURE 8.9   FIGURE 8.10   FIGURE 8.11

4. *Fourth team: Balls and wall*

    Stand eight to twelve feet away from the wall. Throw the ball against the wall and jump over it after the first bounce. Two or three may like to join up one behind the other with each jumping over the ball as it reaches him.

Note: You may prefer to let them practice a skill such as volleyball serve if this has already been taught.

5. *Fifth team: Mat and Cane*

Two children hold the cane about a foot above the ground in front of a mat. Their task is to jump over the cane and roll on the mat. Children may go two at a time. Some may take their weight straight on to their arms and "go over" while others will jump over, land on their feet, then roll. The height of the cane can be raised or lowered according to the ability of the individual performers.

Make sure that the children are aware that *they* and not *you* are responsible for the sensible use of the cane.

6. *Sixth team: Mat*

Jump off the stage and on to the mat, then go straight into a roll.

If there are children who find the stage too high, let them use their hands as they jump off.

Teaching Points

Some classes may be able to get out apparatus and have a turn on each piece of equipment in the first lesson. The fact that everybody has actually arranged his own and knows what to do with their apparatus, however, is the most important thing. You may wish to let two teams get themselves organized first while the rest watch and you comment, then two more teams, and so on. There will be little time for more than this for the first lesson. It will take much less time in the next lesson to arrange apparatus, thus allowing more time for practice and to begin to rotate after five minutes at each station.

Watch the children's forward rolls and make sure that they are tucking their heads under and taking their weight on the back of the neck and shoulders. (See Part II, Lesson Three.)

The above apparatus arrangements were selected with three things in mind. These are:

1. To give the children an opportunity to land from a variety of heights and to learn to control their landing and rolling action.
2. To present movement tasks which are sufficiently challenging to the more skillful children and, at the same time, to provide opportunities for the less skilled to perform tasks which are within the limitations of their own abilities.
3. To give an opportunity for some original thought and inventiveness. Emphasize the point that not only is there an individual challenge for each child to perform to the highest standard of which he is capable, but there is a challenge to each group to see if they can work independently and yet with consideration for each other. You will be keeping an eye on everyone but visiting the groups that need your help the most.

If the teams rotate to three or four different stations, each team leader in turn must remember (and you may write down) which place they should start at next lesson. Apparatus away, and line up or simply go and get changed. Your first lesson is over. Each time it will be easier and more rewarding.

Lesson Reminder for Lesson No. 1

PART I: INTRODUCTORY ACTIVITY
  Running with variations in direction *or* "musical hoops."

PART II: MOVEMENT TRAINING
  Backward diagonal rolls.

PART III: APPARATUS WORK
1. Bench inclined on wallbar.
2. Benches and mat for "storming" (see photograph in Lesson 3).
3. Passing on box.
4. Balls against wall.
5. Cane and Mat.
6. Mat and Stage.
Note: Where you do not have sufficient apparatus, look through other primary and intermediate apparatus diagrams and adapt or invent your own variations.

DIAGRAM L: Suggested Apparatus Arrangement for Lesson No. 1

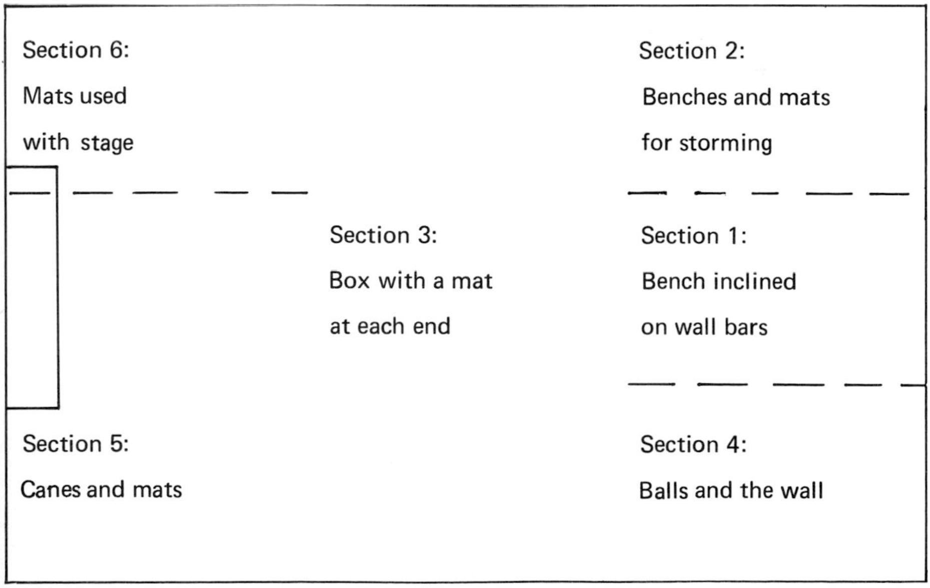

Section 6: Mats used with stage	Section 2: Benches and mats for storming
	Section 3: Box with a mat at each end	Section 1: Bench inclined on wall bars
Section 5: Canes and mats	Section 4: Balls and the wall

Lesson No. 2

It may be necessary for some classes to repeat the first lesson. Other classes who react quickly and easily should proceed with Lesson No. 2.

Part I: Introductory Activity

Same as Lesson No. 1. Use the alternate Introductory Activity suggested in Lesson No. 1.

Part II: Movement Training

1. Practice rocking forward and backward.
2. Practice backward diagonal rolls.
3. Introduce the sideways "tucked roll" by asking the children to lie on their sides with knees bent, elbows tucked in, forming a "curled-up position." Gently rock from one side to the other. After a few turns, increase the momentum and roll right over. This is a sideways tucked roll. The teacher should explain to the children that this is the main protective roll they should use when they lose their balance, or trip, or fall, or when dropping from a height. Allow time for practice.

As a break from rolling on the floor: "Let me see your handstands! It does not matter if you cannot get right up; go as high as you can." "How quietly can you bring your feet down?"

Teaching Points

Make sure that all the children know that in order to maintain their balance during a handstand, the back of the neck should be "shortened" by lifting the head upwards.

FIGURE 8.12   **FIGURE 8.13**   **FIGURE 8.14**

After practicing the handstand, ask the children, as their feet come down from the handstand position, to "over-balance," then go straight into a sideways tucked roll. Allow time for practice and find someone to demonstrate. A short final practice, and instruct the children to practice this movement in the first few minutes of the next lesson, (as soon as they come into the gymnasium).

Part III: Apparatus Work

Same as Lesson No. 1. Continue rotation of groups until each has had a turn on each set of apparatus.

The team working on the bench inclined on the wall bars could now divide into two groups—one going *up* the bench and *down* the wall bars, passing the group going in the opposite direction as they come toward them, without touching.

Lesson No. 3

Continue from Lesson No. 2.

Part I: Introductory Activity

A slight variation on "musical hoops" at this time. Ask the children to decide upon three different positions. For example, position (1) is standing in the hoop on one leg; position (2) is placing hands in the hoop and feet

FIGURE 8.15

FIGURE 8.16

outside the hoop; and position (3) is curled up in the middle of the hoop with weight on both feet. Instead of saying "change," you call out *one* of the three numbers. Thus, the children have to think of *how* they must arrive in the hoop, as well as being quick to find one. The "last" child, as well as all children who get into the wrong position, have a penalty (any task thought up by the class, providing the latter is "in fun" and not a serious punishment).

FIGURE 8.17

Teaching Points
Review points under Lesson No. 2.

Part II: Movement Training
Practice backward rolls, sideways tuck rolls, and handstand into sideways roll.

Part III: Apparatus Work
When children have learned to land from a height and can go straight into a forward roll, try:
1. Turning in the air and going into a backward diagonal roll.
2. Turning sideways and going into a sideways tucked roll.

Lesson No. 4

Continue from Lesson No. 3.

Part I: Introductory Activity
Same as Lesson No. 3 with the possibility of adding one or two different "positions."

Part II: Movement Training
Practice the backward diagonal roll and when the children get all their weight on their feet again, suggest that they think of another way of returning to the starting position. The addition of a specific object such as a small mat or beanbag can be used to act as a focus to go over backward one way, and return a different way. Some examples of returning a different way could be, sideways roll, forward roll, broad jump, jump on to hands (cat springs) cartwheel, or a hop. Give children enough time to work out their own response but be ready to suggest a movement to those who seem to be devoid of any ideas.

FIGURE 8.18

FIGURE 8.19

Part III: Apparatus Work

A simple rearrangement of apparatus (see layout in Lesson No. 1) will stimulate new and varied movements. However, avoid a complete rearrangement of all apparatus in one lesson. Begin with one or two groups then allow others to change during the next lesson.

Some rearrangements and movement variation may be as follows:

1. Wall bars and a mat: Climb up wall bars to a height comfortable for you and cross over to the other side. Leap off and go straight into a sideways tucked roll on landing. If you have no wall bars improvise with strong boxes and chairs of different sizes.

2. Two benches and a large mat: One half of the team stands on each bench. The mat is placed between the two benches. Develop a continuous pattern involving the two groups. Each group jumps off their bench, rolls on the mat and jumps up on the other bench. Each participant must avoid touching the other, particularly those coming from the opposite bench.

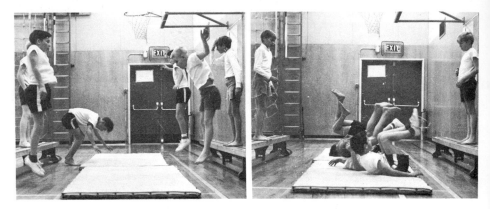

FIGURE 8.20   **FIGURE 8.21**

3. Box and mats: Same as Lesson No. 1. Have you tried three different ways of passing?
4. Balls and wall: Develop any idea that may have been produced or tell the team to work out a throw, bounce and catch type sequence which they must teach to the next team when it is time to rotate. Use hoops if desired.
5. Mat and two canes: The two children who hold a cane for the rest of the team to jump over may now be given two canes. If they hold one high and the other low, they will create a "window" which can be varied in height according to individual needs again.
6. Mat and stage: Add two rolls on landing. Make the two rolls different.

FIGURE 8.22

Lesson No. 5

Part I: Introductory Activity

This should be brief since most of the time allowed for this lesson should be spent on Movement Training. Ask the children to run anywhere in the gymnasium, slowly at first, then gain speed. Stress that they should weave in and out of each other, and use the whole gymnasium. When you say "stop," they should freeze into a stationary position.

It might be fun to have the children drop down quickly into a "crouch position" or go right down on their tummies when you say "stop." Look for the last head to "disappear" from your sight.

Part II: Movement Training

Join up with a partner and work out a simple sequence together involving rocking and rolling and returning to the original starting position. An example of this might be:

1. Rock backward and forward.
2. Rock backward into a diagonal roll, then
3. Jump forward on to hands.

FIGURE 8.23

OR

1. Lie curled up on one side.
2. Roll over on to the other side and stretch out into a log roll.
3. Roll over once completely, then lift weight on to hands and feet in a "push-up" position; then
4. Return to original place by "turning turtle"—(keep weight on hands and feet, and rotate as you *walk* so that tummy faces floor, ceiling, then floor).

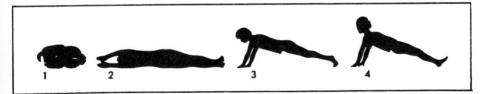

FIGURE 8.24

Part III: Apparatus Work

Same as previous lesson.

Assessment of Previous Lessons

The previous lessons should represent a progression of achievement. Obviously, the speed with which they are completed depends upon the unique abilities of the class and the teacher. Hence, a teacher may, if she believes it necessary, repeat any lesson as often as she wishes. The children's interest will be maintained if they catch the teacher's enthusiasm and *know toward what they are working.*

Let us now consider how much has been accomplished during the past five lessons.

1. The teacher and the class should be completely familiar with the format of the lesson. Both should feel there is never enough time.
2. The children should realize that they are expected to think as well as move.
3. The children should realize that although this approach is fun, they are expected to work hard.
4. The children should understand that you are concerned about how and where they move and that self-discipline is required during every part of each lesson.
5. The children should realize it is possible to roll on the floor without hurting themselves and that they should automatically finish any "landing from height" with a roll.
6. All should understand the idea of sequence building, (linking two or three movements together).
7. The children should be able to get out the apparatus quickly and quietly and to begin to work after the teacher or the team leader makes sure all safety measures have been checked.
8. The teacher should have established the procedure of allowing skillful movements or interesting ideas to be demonstrated. This is particularly important on the apparatus. The latter provides each team rotating on to new apparatus to have the image (if there is one) of someone's performance as a standard to work to or from.

CHAPTER NINE

Theme Two: Adding to the Range and Understanding of Movement

Adding to the range and understanding of movement is sometimes referred to as "Body Awareness." The basic aims of this second theme are to stretch the children's imagination, to make them discover the many different parts of themselves on which they can balance and move. To encourage children to develop a movement vocabulary by helping them invent and practice simple movement sequences, and to use a partner to help a movement by acting as a support or by complementing a pattern.

Lesson No. 1

Part I: Introductory Activity (Imaginative Manipulation of Balls)

Instruct the children to take a ball and bounce it with one hand as they walk anywhere in the gymnasium. Next alternate one hand and then the other. When their spacing is good and they are moving in and out of each other with good ball control, ask them "What other part of you can make the ball bounce?" Children may try elbows, head, fists, knees. Select a good example and allow all children to attempt to do the same. If this produces no ideas, ask them to bounce the ball to get a high rebound, then head it gently and control it again by the hand. Make this continuous. Now think of a different sequence.

Part II: Movement Training

After putting the balls away, have each child find a space on the floor and sit down. Now, "Find a position where you can balance on three parts of your body. Can you balance on three different parts? Now can you remember your first position? If so, try to move smoothly from the first to the second position." Look for children who have immediately taken some difficult and interesting positions. This may stimulate those who cannot think

of anything beyond two feet and one hand. Continue by saying, "Now balance with your weight on two parts—two different parts. Can you now move from three to two then finish in your second position of three?"

FIGURE 9.1

Part III: Apparatus Work
1. Wall bars: Combine with a partner to make two alphabet letters on the wall bars.
2. Benches: (two) Go from one end of the bench to another in a variety of ways, keeping your weight on two parts of you. On the second crossing, try three parts.

   Mats: Find two balance positions and link them with a roll.
   OR
3. Box: At a comfortable height with no spring board. Use hands to get on and off the box. Finally, get on and then off the box without using hands.
4. Hoops and individual mats or softball bases: Stand a hoop vertically by placing an individual mat through it. In this way two or more hoops may be placed so that they form a tunnel. Go through and over the hoops without touching them.
5. Balls and hoops: Divide the group into sets of three with a ball and a hoop per group. Ask the children to "invent a game." They may use more balls or hoops if they wish.

FIGURE 9.2   **FIGURE 9.3**

6. Stage and two canes and mat or jumping stands and rope: Two people (or jumping stand) hold a cane a little below the level of the stage and a foot or two away from it. A second cane is placed at the end of the mat supported on boxes or chairs not far from the ground. They jump from the stage over the first cane, roll on the mat and use their arms and go over the second cane. Can you add a balance of your own to the sequence?

Lesson Reminder for Lesson No. 1

PART I: INTRODUCTORY ACTIVITY

Bouncing ball freely—stationary and moving. "Can you bounce it with a different part of you?"

PART II: MOVEMENT TRAINING

Balancing on three parts: three different parts.
Balancing on two parts: two different parts.
Link if time.

FIGURE 9.4

FIGURE 9.5

FIGURE 9.6

PART III: APPARATUS WORK
1. Alphabet letters on wall bars.
2. Moving along benches on three and two parts.
3. On and off box with hands; on and off box with no hands; or linking balancing and rolling.
4. Through and over hoops held vertically, by small mats or baseball bases.
5. Original ball game in threes with hoop.
6. Stage, cane, mat, jumping stands and rope. From stage jump over rope on to mat, roll and over cane in any way.

FIGURE 9.7

DIAGRAM M: Suggested Apparatus Arrangement for Lesson No. 1

Section 2:

2 Benches

— — — — — — — — —

Section 3:   Section 1:

Section 6:

Box and mat   Cave or

Jumping stands

with ropes across.   wall bars

Mats and

canes balanced on   Section 5:

chairs

Balls and hoops

Section 4:

Hoops and small mats

Lesson No. 2

Part I: Introductory Activity

Instruct the children to bounce a ball as they walk or run anywhere in the gymnasium. "Bounce it or toss it with any part of you and any way you like but control it." This may be done on the spot or moving. "Choose three of your ideas and put them together into a sequence."

Part II: Movement Training

After the balls are put away ask the children to find a partner. "Teach your partner the sequence you made up in this or the last lesson." Decide which one you like best or invent a new one, then perform the sequence together "making matching movements."

FIGURE 9.8

Part III: Apparatus Work

Same as previous lesson. With the group using the hoops ask them to use the edge of the hoop and balance on three then four parts of their bodies, link the two movements smoothly, then "roll out" of the hoop.

Lesson No. 3

Part I: Introductory Activity

1. Move around the gym on two hands and one foot (not too long).
2. On two hands and two feet.
3. Keep your hands still while your feet move and vice versa.
4. As you do this can you find a position from which you can roll and return to your hands—feet position. Now a different way?

Part II: Movement Training

Allow children to complete their balance sequence from the previous lesson. Stress that the sequence should be smooth and as polished as they can make it. A further challenge could be "keep one part of you in contact with your partner." Next try a different part.

Part III: Apparatus Work

Same as previous lesson.

Lesson Nos. 4 and 5 (Bridges)

Part I: Introductory Activity

Same as previous lesson.

Part II: Movement Training

Ask children to join up with a partner. One of the partners makes a "bridge" shape and the other sees how many ways he can travel over, under, or through. "Change positions with your partner, and repeat the movement task." Attempt to get the children to develop (and show good examples) of difficult or original bridge shapes. Also, encourage variety in the way each partner goes through each "bridge" by asking them to change directions, or move through the bridges without letting their hands touch the floor.

FIGURE 9.9   FIGURE 9.10

Part III: Apparatus Work

1. Same as previous lesson but make a bridge on the *wall bars* for your partner to go through.
2. Make bridges somewhere as you go along the *benches*.

FIGURE 9.11   **FIGURE 9.12**

3. Make a bridge for a partner during or after your work on the *box*.
4. Same as previous lesson.
5. Make two different bridge shapes over your own ball—then set it rolling gently and try to follow it making a series of bridge-like shapes.
6. Same as previous lesson.

Lesson Reminder for Lessons 4 and 5

PART I: INTRODUCTORY ACTIVITY
   Traveling on two hands and one foot; then feet still, hands move, and vice versa, incorporate roll.

PART II: MOVEMENT TRAINING
   Bridges in twos.

PART III: APPARATUS WORK
   Bridge idea in twos applied to:
1. Wall bars (could combine with letter shapes in sequence form).
2. Benches.
3. Box or mats.
4. Hoops.
5. Ball game.
6. Stage, rope, mat, cane.

Lesson No. 6 (Feet High)

Part I: Introductory Activity

In this movement challenge, children are asked to think of a way of moving on the floor keeping one foot higher than any other part of the body. This could be done sliding along on the back and keeping one foot high, or on two hands and one foot with the other held high. Also, cartwheels or handstands appropriately meet this challenge.

Choose two or three different ideas from the children, and have them demonstrate, then let everyone try again.

Part II: Movement Training

Request children to find their own space on the floor, and from their own choice of starting position lift one leg high. Change this starting position and lift the *same* leg high again. Allow them to practice on their own for a while. In the meantime circulate around the gymnasium and look for good ideas. "Look around and try out someone else's ideas."

FIGURE 9.13

Part III: Apparatus Work

For groups one to four, same as previous lesson, but the theme now requires all the groups to get either one or both feet high at some point of their work.

1. Ropes: For feet high, (upside down position using one or two ropes). When waiting for turns practice bridge shapes over balls.
2. Change from the stage to one or two benches inclined on the scaffolding of the baseketball posts.
3. Box: Feet high in middle of vault or on getting off.

FIGURE 9.14   **FIGURE 9.15**

General Comment
By now no one should be idly waiting in a line for a turn. Remind children that if they find this happening to them, they can be practicing handstands or headstands against the wall or bouncing a ball and jumping over or running underneath it. Everybody should be busy!

Lesson Reminder for Lesson No. 6

PART I: INTRODUCTORY ACTIVITY
Moving freely with one or both feet high. Try two different ways. Can you link them with a roll?

PART II: MOVEMENT TRAINING
Lift one foot high, change starting position and lift the same foot high. Link into simple sequence if time.

PART III: APPARATUS WORK
Feet high, at all sections.
1. Wall bars.
2. Benches—One on top of another, children sit on ends to stabilize them.
3. Box—Feet high in middle of vault or on getting off.
                          or
Mats—Use a partner to help get one or two feet high.
4. Vertical hoops—May also be held horizontally by a partner.
5. Ropes instead of balls and hoops.
6. Inclined bench on scaffolding of basketball ring.

DIAGRAM N: Suggested Apparatus Arrangement for Lesson No. 6

Section 2:

Benches

Section 3:

Box and mat

Section 4:

Hoops

Section 5:

Ropes

Section 1:

Cave or wall

bars

Section 6:

Benches inclined on

scaffolding of basket

ball standard

Lesson No. 7

Part I: Introductory Activity

Take a partner and practice "wheelbarrows." One partner has her hands on the floor and lifts one leg up for her partner to hold firmly. When she is balanced the other leg is lifted as well, and they are ready to go. Be very sure to warn the children who are on their feet *not* to push, but simply to support their partner's legs. After a few seconds change partners. Next, ask the children to move in a different way, remembering that one or both legs must become the highest point at some stage in their traveling.

Those experiencing difficulty may like to try a run, turn in the air, land and go straight into a backward rock and finish with both feet in the high air with the hands supporting the hips.

Part II: Movement Training

With your partner find a position where one person has a "foot high" and the other partner helps to support or complete the "shape." Try different ways and experiment with other positions.

Part III: Apparatus Work

Same as previous lesson.

FIGURE 9.16   **FIGURE 9.17**   **FIGURE 9.18**

Lesson Reminder for Lesson No. 7

PART I: INTRODUCTORY ACTIVITY
Wheelbarrows in twos, then own ideas of moving with or without partner with feet high.

From a wheelbarrow position it is easy to help tip the "working" partner into a forward roll.

PART II: MOVEMENT TRAINING
Find two positions where one of the two partners takes "feet high" and the other supports her physically or complements the shape.

PART III: APPARATUS WORK
Same as Lesson No. 6.

Lesson Nos. 8, 9 and 10

In the previous lessons, the children should have been rotating during the apparatus part of the lesson, but quite often and particularly in a forty minute lesson there is only a concern for experimentation involvement and practice, but not too much concern for "finish" or refinement. According to the class and length of lesson, it may be necessary to have the children spend the next three lessons working on the same piece of apparatus in order to produce a more polished individual or group response or "performance." For each of these lessons you may like to give a brief introductory activity and leave out Movement Training in order to move directly to the Apparatus Work.

Teaching Points

1. Encourage the children to analyze carefully what they are doing in order to make sure that they are fully aware of how each movement could be improved.
2. Where possible, encourage the idea of linking movements to form sequences on the floor or on apparatus.
3. Constantly encourage thoughtful rearrangement of apparatus or additions of small apparatus where the children have a specific idea in mind. Sometimes, however, children spend so much time rearranging apparatus they virtually have no time to do anything constructive.
4. Encourage imaginative and original ideas which sometimes get lost from sight in the enthusiasm of the moment.

Assessment of Previous Lessons

Before moving on to the next theme, let us review our achievements. By this stage the children should be full of ideas and feel confident that the teacher will notice when they produce a "response" that is really noteworthy. All children should be accustomed to balancing and moving with their weight on a variety of parts. They should have become accustomed to the idea that a partner can be used as a support, as an obstacle, and to complement a shape or pattern as well as to "match movements" and help in the invention of ideas. Further, most childern should have started to think about shape and design and how their bodies can indicate the pattern they are thinking of, and how two people extend the scope of the design considerably.

As with safety training, move on to Theme Three if you feel ready. If you are having fun developing some of the previous ideas with your children, don't rush them, there is plenty of time. Do you feel more confident yourself?

TEN

Theme Three: Stretching and Curling

Since so many gymnastic activities come under the heading of stretching and curling, or produce a stretched or curled shape, we find ourselves with an extremely broad theme. However, once the children have discovered some of the ways they can adapt the ideas embodied in this theme to floor, partner, and apparatus work, we shall attempt to make their work more sophisticated by introducing variations in direction (forward, backward, sideways, and diagonal) as well as high, medium, and low levels and variations of speed.

The sequences which children have been developing to this point have probably not involved the linking of more than three to four movements. By the end of this theme it is expected that sequences should be as long or short as their "authors" or inventors wish them to be. Children in the intermediate grades can have very long movement memories, when the pattern or sequence has been their own creation and they are given sufficient time to work on them.

Lesson No. 1

Part I: Introductory Activity

If individual mats are available, place them in a staggered position down the middle of the gymnasium. All the children then go to the side of the room facing their own mat. (Beanbags could be used as a substitute.)

Ask them to run and leap over their mats. If the class is large it will be easier for the children to run and leap from the same direction and walk back again. This will remove the possibility of head-on collisions. Emphasize a strong push from the back leg, chest and head lifted high. This should give a feeling of *stretch* and flight. Care must be taken to insure a controlled landing, with resilience rather than bending of the "landing" leg.

Now having *felt* the stretch involved in a leap, we now turn our attentions to the contrasting idea of our theme—"curling."

This time instead of walking back to leap again, have the children stand a short distance away from the mat, then crouch down and jump on to their hands (in a "cat spring") getting their hands in the middle of the mat. This requires considerable strength of arm and shoulder girdle. Also, the feet should push the body into the air before the arms catch the weight of the body. After this initial spring there should be a quick curl as the knees are tucked underneath the body.

After a few turns of the cat spring, combine the two ideas, that is, leaping over the mat and cat-spring back.

FIGURE 10.1   FIGURE 10.2

Part II: Movement Training

Ask the class to find a space on the floor and curl up in any position. "From this position, stretch out into any stretched position and return to your curled position. Repeat and try to get a better and fuller stretch, before returning. Now find a different curled position and stretch out and return again. Can you go smoothly from your first curled position to your first stretch, and then return to your second curled position and finally go straight into your second stretch position?" Thus we have four movements involving stretch-curl-stretch-curl.

Point out the children you think show skill and originality, smoothness in transitions, and clearness of shape.

Give a few more minutes for children to practice getting a smooth *flow* as they link one movement to another, and a feeling of total stretch, and its opposite rounding.

FIGURE 10.3   FIGURE 10.4

Part III: Apparatus Work

1. Southhampton Cave pulled out and parallel bars put up at hip height: Balance on top of bar in a stretch position, curl fingers underneath and do a forward roll off, keeping knees curled tight up to chest and try not to make any noise as your feet touch the ground. After you have practiced this, can you think of any other stretched positions or curled positions using the bar?
2. Two benches inclined on basketball scaffolding: (See photograph on page 163) Invent a way of going up and down, stretching and curling, *or* benches arranged in the following way:
   a. Broad side up.
   b. Narrow side up on top of first.
   c. Inclined by hooks on narrow side of second.
   d. Fourth bench, if available, inclined down the opposite side (see Figure 12.3 for "Bridges," page 188).
      Lie on stomach or back in a good stretch position, pull yourself along by your arms, hands and feet, crawling in a curled position along the narrow side of the bench and either jump off or go down the other bench with a strong sliding pull.
3. Mats: Any sequence involving rolls, headstands, handstands, or cartwheels.
   or
   Box: Less two layers: Forward roll on top of box (curl) feet on the end and a high spring off (stretch). Can you do this a different way? Practice the first way and any other way that you have thought of.
4. Springboard and mat: Run, and with two foot takeoff at the end of the board, *stretch* in the air and go into a roll, on landing (*curl*).
5. Ropes: Reach up and grasp the rope then stretch backward or sideways, following by a curled position (bring knees up) and finish with a swing. Those waiting for a turn practice bridge and cartwheel shapes over a slow rolling ball.
6. Stage with mat hanging over the edge and another mat on the floor: Make up a simple sequence involving stretching and curling, using headstands, handstands, and rolls.

DIAGRAM O:　Suggested Apparatus Arrangement for Lesson No. 1

Section 4:

Spring board

and mat

Section 1:

CAVE or

parallel bars

— — — — —

Section 6:

Mat hanging over

stage, second mat on floor.

Section 3:

Box and mat

Section 2:

balance beams

— — — —　　　　　　　— — — — —

Section 5:

Ropes, balls

and hoop

Section 2:

Bench, inclined on

basketball scaffolding

Lesson Reminder for Lesson No. 1

PART I:　INTRODUCTORY ACTIVITY
Leap over small mat (or any piece of small apparatus). Cat-spring back.

PART II:　MOVEMENT TRAINING
Stretch-curl sequence from different parting positions.

PART III:　APPARATUS WORK
1. Parallel bar on Cave.
2. Bench inclined on basketball
　　　　　or
Mats or handstand—rolling sequence.
3. Box—Roll and spring off—then own variations.
4. Springboard and mat—Jump with a real S-T-R-E-T-C-H, land and roll.
5. Ropes—Make yourself as small and round as possible, then stretch. Use single or double ropes.
6. Stage with mat handling plus one on floor. Rolls, handstands, etc.

Lesson No. 2

Part I: Introductory Activity

Have the children practice leaping over mat and cat-spring back, then do a different leap over and roll back. Practice several times remembering to stretch fully and curl tightly.

Part II: Movement Training

Ask children to join up with a partner and make up a sequence of at least four movements involving stretching and curling. They may face each other or be side by side.

FIGURE 10.5   **FIGURE 10.6**   **FIGURE 10.7**

FIGURE 10.8   **FIGURE 10.9**

Teaching Points

Move freely about the gymnasium giving children the feeling that you are watching all of them and will be able to help or suggest an idea to those in need.

Part III: Apparatus Work

Same as previous lesson.

Lesson No. 3 (Sub-theme Variation of Speed)

Part I: Introductory Activity

Same as previous lesson. Draw upon ideas from the class.

Part II: Movement Training

Allow children to practice the sequence they have developed with their partner. Next, ask them to do it all as slowly as they can. Next do it as quickly as they can. Finally, do some parts slowly and some parts quickly.

Part III: Apparatus Work

Same as previous lesson.

Lesson No. 4

Part I: Introductory Activity

Same as previous lesson.

Part II: Movement Training

Practice sequences emphasizing a change of speed as well as the *flow* of one movement into the next.

Part III: Apparatus Work

Same as previous lesson.

Try to get the children to give a variation of speed in their apparatus work by deciding which part could best be done quickly and which part done slowly. For example, on the box a slow roll could precede a quick explosive jump off the box. Every section should be able to show some change of speed.

Lesson No. 5

Part I: Introductory Activity

Ask the children to take any stretched or curled-up position on the floor. "Can you move in this position?" Find a way of moving while maintaining a curled position. Do the same in a stretch position. Work out a way of moving involving stretching and curling alternatively.

FIGURE 10.10

Alternate Introductory Activity

If children are not prepared to be this informal, use the following Alternate Introductory Activity.

Ask the children to take a hoop and start rolling it anywhere in the gymnasium. They must keep it close to themselves and not let it bump into anyone or anyone else's hoop. They should look for the spaces to move into as quickly as they can. "Change after a little while and think of something else to do with your hoop. If you like, you may join up with a partner and perform something together while in motion or do something on the spot." Allow the children to practice freely but look for ideas that you could build around your next Introductory Activity. It should, of course, involve stretching and curling.

FIGURE 10.11

Part II: Movement Training

If you have used the Alternate Introductory Activity, leave Movement Training and go straight to the Apparatus Work. (The alternate introductory activity covers both very well.)

If you used the first Introductory Activity, then include the following Movement Training.

Alternate Movement Training

The movement training part of this lesson should include:
1. Practice quick and slow sequences with your partner.
2. Using a hoop, see if you can adapt your partner sequence to fit into either the middle, the outer edge, or simply use the hoop as an obstacle as you perform your sequence.

FIGURE 10.12   **FIGURE 10.13**   **FIGURE 10.14**

Part III: Apparatus Work

Same as previous lesson. Keep within the theme of stretching and curling.

FIGURE 10.15   **FIGURE 10.16**

The above shows an idea developed by Grade Four. All jump "astride" on to the box in very quick succession (the first ones quickly moving forward in cowboy style). Each then developed a distinctive way of "dismounting"—(cartwheels, forward and backward rolls, and jumps) in "slow motion."

Lesson Reminder for Lesson No. 5

PART I: INTRODUCTORY ACTIVITY
Stretch—curl moving *or* rolling hoop, then own ideas.

PART II: MOVEMENT TRAINING
Adapt sequence in pairs to a hoop.

PART III: APPARATUS WORK
This should be the same as previous lessons; however, ideas should begin to be generated by the children. Although the Apparatus sections appear to be the same, many different approaches should be forthcoming.

Remember to visit each section over a period of two lessons. Sometimes one becomes too involved with one particular group needing guidance, resulting in unintentional neglect of the other groups.

Lesson Nos. 6, 7, 8 and 9

Part I: Introductory Activity

Allow the children to practice any activity with a hoop. If the class is imaginative you will have no difficulty in finding many new and different ways of using a hoop. At your discretion, select a few good ideas for demonstration, then allow the whole class to practice these new movements.

With some classes a review of Introductory Activities might be to have the hoops scattered freely on the floor and use a different version of musical hoops. For example, when you say "curl," the class must jump into the hoop in a curled position and vice versa for "stretch." Later they could move freely over the hoops stretching (leaping or jumping) and curling, jumping with a "tuck" or rolling.

Part II: Movement Training

A combined "class sequence." This is a very helpful method of getting some classes to build movement sequences if they do not have much confidence or a large "movement vocabulary." With a partner and a hoop each pair work out a good starting position from which a sequence could be built. The teacher then chooses which position she thinks would be the best. The child then demonstrates this starting position to everyone.

Everybody now works out what would be a suitable or interesting position to move into from the starting position, bearing in mind our theme of stretch and curl. The teacher then chooses which second position she likes. Again a demonstration and class practice.

This, of course, continues until you have a relatively long sequence. It is therefore the product of both the class and yourself. When everybody knows what they are doing, they should practice it during the next few lessons to get it as polished as they can. Consider the shape, position and movement of every part of the body, including fingers and toes, and show a variation of speed.

Part III: Apparatus Work

If the children are feeling unhappy or unable to work out ideas sufficiently challenging, very often a rearrangement of the apparatus or the addition of small apparatus will provide the necessary stimulus. At this stage of the theme, you may like to let the children go straight to their apparatus after the Introductory Activity and concentrate for a few lessons on one of two areas in order to work out their ideas in greater depth and to a higher standard of performance. Do not forget simple additional challenges such as moving in the opposite direction, going over or under as well as around, or pass a partner without touching.

Grade Seven decided upon this "E-N-D" to the theme of stretch and curl for our films. From a tight curled position, they alternately moved quickly or slowly to form each letter of T-H-E E-N-D!

FIGURE 10.17
FIGURE 10.18

ELEVEN

Theme Four:
Change of Direction

Directions do not have to be taught in the intermediate grades as they do in the primary grades. The idea, however, of moving in different ways in a variety of directions in a sequence will help to develop further understanding of movement, and will give greater form and pattern to all subsequent sequences.

The ideas involving direction in this theme may evolve from any movement, such as, from jumps, rolls, or handstands. The choice of movement may be left to the children. The limitation set by the teacher is to show a change of direction.

FIGURE 11.1

This theme will be more effectively understood by the children if they work with a partner or a small apparatus in order to give them an object to move around or avoid, prior to changing direction.

Lesson No. 1

Part I: Introductory Activity

Start this activity by having the children run anywhere in the gymnasium, and leap over the painted lines on the floor. Stress that they should not bump into anyone.

When you say "change," they should run backwards. Then "change" again, they turn and run forwards. Next time have them run sideways and when you say "change"—and ask them "What sort of action can move you sideways easily?" "Could you work out a different type of 'run' for the forward, backward, and sideways changes?" Finally when you call "change," allow the class to choose which direction they will move and in their own way.

Part: II: Movement Training

With an object (mat or beanbag) have the children work out a jumping pattern using clear directions such as forward, backward, and sideways with any sort of hop, jump, skip, or a combination of all three.

Part III: Apparatus Work

1. Southhampton Cave: (with ladder) Place one parallel bar at knee height and the other at head height. "Travel up ladder and along bars showing a change of direction as you go. For example, go backwards, forwards, and sideways at different stages."
   Mats: Show a series of rolls in a variety of directions.
   or
2. Box and two benches, side by side: "Think of ways of going along the benches, changing direction. Begin with a forward vault on to the box and get off in a sideways directional movement."
3. Three benches: Two benches are in a "V" formation with the third bench narrow side up, lying on top of and across the first two benches. Play tag with a beanbag but make sure the benches are stable or play follow the leader showing changes of direction as you go.
4. Canes and chairs or boxes: Arrange the canes, preferably at different heights and a good distance between them. Under and over with a change of direction.

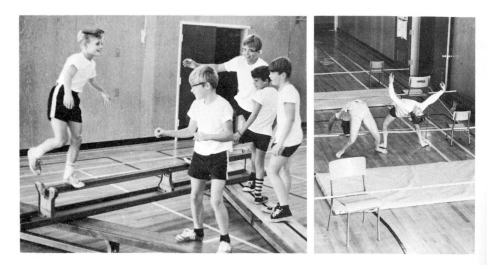

FIGURE 11.2   **FIGURE 11.3**

5. Hoops and Pins: Balance each hoop horizontally on three bowling pins. "Go in and out showing a change of direction—in and out might be thought of as under and over."

6. Springboard, stage mats: Place the springboard about two feet away from the stage with two large or several small mats on the stage. Run in threes with the person in the center using the springboard to jump from, placing his hands on the stage and going straight into a roll. The outer two run, jump, turn, and sit on the platform and go straight into a backward diagonal roll.

   Note: If you wish to form two extra groups in the interest of greater individuality and more "turns" for each child, the following may be helpful.

7. Ropes: Climb *up* one rope as far as you can, reach *sideways* and transfer to the next one and come *down*.

8. Any spare mat: Two children could work out different kinds of rolls, cartwheels, and could make an excellent direction sequence out of this type of activity.

Lesson Reminder for Lesson No. 1

PART I: INTRODUCTORY ACTIVITY

   Moving in different ways in different directions.

PART II: MOVEMENT TRAINING

   Jumping directional sequence over mat or beanbag.

PART III: APPARATUS WORK

1. Southhampton Cave with ladder attachment.
2. Box and two benches side by side leading toward box. Jumps, or rolls, etc. showing change of direction on to the box facing forward—get off sideways.
3. Tag on benches.
4. Canes and chairs. Under and over with change of direction.
5. Hoops balanced on bowling pins.

FIGURE 11.4   **FIGURE 11.5**

6. Jumping on to the stage with a turn into a backward diagonal roll. Those children who are not comfortable jumping on to the stage from the spring-board can run and jump on to the stage with a turn. They are then in a good position to swing back into a backward diagonal roll.
7. Ropes—Up and change to next rope and down.
8. Mat—Practice sequences.

DIAGRAM P: Suggested Apparatus Arrangement for Lesson No. 1

Section 4:	Section 2:	Section 8:
Canes on chairs	2 benches leading to box large mat at side of box	Large mat
Section 6:	Section 5:	Section 1:
Springboard	Hoops balanced on pins	CAVE or parallel bars. Section 2. balance beams with inclined ladder.
Section 7:		Section 3:
Ropes		2 or 3 benches with narrow side up.

Lesson No. 2

Part I: Introductory Activity

Children are to select any movement, then travel in a forward direction. The teacher chooses which idea she likes, then all children practice this movement. The same with backward and sideway movements, thus everyone in the class will perform the same movement when the teacher directs "forward, backward, or sideways."

FIGURE 11.6

Part: II: Movement Training

Take the same object as last lesson, that is, a beanbag or mat and use your arms to take the weight of the body as you make your directional pattern. This might progress along the following lines:

Cat spring over beanbag *forward*, roll *backward*, jump from side to side, both feet together in a forward direction and a cartwheel diagonally back again.

Part III: Apparatus Work

Same as previous lesson.

Lesson No. 3

Part I: Introductory Activity

Same as previous lesson. Children should now change direction, keeping the same movements decided upon in the previous lesson without the teacher having to call out a change of direction. The choice of direction should be dictated by the general spacing in the room.

Part: II: Movement Training

Allow children to take a partner and a beanbag. "Make up a simple directional sequence over the beanbag. Do the same movements, that is, match movements with your partner. Begin facing each other."

FIGURE 11.7

Part III: Apparatus Work

Same as previous lesson.

Lesson No. 4

Part I: Introductory Activity

Ask the children to skip anywhere in the gymnasium with their own rope. Watch for spacing.

Part: II: Movement Training

Join up with your partner and put your ropes stretched out side by side with about one foot between them. Make up a series of movements which involve changing places with your partner. The following delightful sequences were created by a Grade Six class.

| **FIGURE 11.8** | **FIGURE 11.9** | **FIGURE 11.10** |

Some children added mats, but the sequence still involved changing places and changing directions.

And, still greater variations:

| **FIGURE 11.11** | **FIGURE 11.12** | **FIGURE 11.13** |

FIGURE 11.14 FIGURE 11.15 FIGURE 11.16 FIGURE 11.17

As we mentioned before, if the teacher finds the children have produced some interesting ideas which deviate from the initial idea, she should not hesitate to develop them as far as she can. As illustrated here:

FIGURE 11.18 FIGURE 11.19 FIGURE 11.20 FIGURE 11.21

Developing ideas consists of allowing children time to explore and experiment and then build movements into a sequence. At this stage of development, extensive opportunity should be given to the children to practice in order to develop the feeling of "finish."

General Comments

At this stage it may be wise to briefly return to Safety Training with a combination of Flight. Perhaps too, a repeat of the previous two themes with strong emphasis on quick and slow or combine Stretch and Curl with a Direction change.

Are you beginning to see the possibilities of many variations of themes? Do you feel you understand more about movement than you did during the first lesson?

Now, a few ideas on how to tackle a theme of Flight before proceeding to our final theme.

Flight is concerned with the lifting of the body into the air, the way it travels in the air, and the receiving of the body weight back onto the floor.

Leaps and jumps involving:

1. From one foot to one foot.
2. From two feet to one foot.
3. From one foot to two feet.
4. From two feet to two feet.
5. From two feet to the same foot.
6. From feet to hands, crouch jumps and cat springs.

A feeling of flight may also be experienced when the arms receive the body weight. The following movement tasks provide preliminary strengthening in the arm and shoulder girdle area.

1. One person holds a hoop horizontally for his partner to jump in, reach over on to the floor, crouch and jump out, taking all his weight on his arms.
2. Travels along the broad side of two benches from side to side taking all their weight on their arms.
3. Place a beanbag between your heels and as you do your crouch jump see if you can flick the beanbag over your head. This also trains the children to keep their feet together.
4. Crouch jump over two benches (one on top of another). Two children will have to take turns at sitting on the ends to stabilize the benches.

FIGURE 11.22

A theme of Flight gives the children an opportunity to go back to safety rolls and jumping from a variety of heights. This will be useful as you can compare the class's performance to their first attempt and see what progress has been made.

From crouch jumps into cat springs into handstands and cartwheels. All these are dependent on strength of the arms and shoulder girdle. On the apparatus, running and jumping on to *ropes*. Leaping on and off the box, using different types of jumps. Running and jumping off inclined *benches*.

FIGURE 11.23

Running and jumping onto the *stage* and leaping off. Leaping over *canes* and jumping on to hands through or over a held cane. All these activities involve takeoff, flight, and landing. A high standard of performance will give confidence a greater feeling for "line" and control of the weight of the body.

On to our final theme—Twisting.

CHAPTER
TWELVE

Theme Five:
Twisting

You may like to incorporate the idea of "turning" as well as "twisting" in this theme, as this will not only give a wider range of movement opportunities but, in addition, will clarify the difference between a twist and a turn.

A twisting action takes place when one part of the body remains in a fixed position and the other part turns as far as it can without altering the position of the fixed part. Turning is a word that is loosely applied to movements which are not strong enough to be called twisting, such as turning one's head to the side. Turning can also mean "about turn" or turning to change direction where there is no twisting at all.

The primary grades can have a great deal of fun with such games as statues and twirling around holding on to a partner, then letting go. After continuing with the momentum of the spin for a few seconds the children freeze into a variety of shapes and at a variety of levels. "Finish with a twisted shape near to the ground," or "finish with one of you high and one low, both in a twisted shape."

Grades Four and Five also have a lot of fun with this activity; however, being larger than primary children they have farther to fall and are normally stiffer though nevertheless stronger at the twirling part of the game. Hence, games involving gentle falling to the ground and a return to safety rolls might be a good place to make a start. One Grade Five class had a lot of fun from "dying" which will be explained in the first lesson plan, and although "statues" is included in the primary lesson plans and not in the intermediate plans, it could be easily introduced *after* the dying game had made them able to fall, relax and roll without hurting themselves.

Lesson No. 1 (Twisting and Turning)

Part I: Introductory Activity

Allow the children to take a ball and practice anything they wish. Now that you have taught the children for some months it should be interesting to observe them with this indirect teaching approach. You should find much greater variety in what the children think of doing with their balls and the natural spacing in the gymnasium as they move. Check any child who hurls a ball across the room and stipulate that whatever he does with his ball, he should keep it within his own reach.

FIGURE 12.1

Now that everyone has had a chance to experiment and you have called attention to any interesting ideas, ask the children to move as quickly as they can all over the floor, and using alternate hands, bounce the ball as they go.

After a while, and when they are accustomed to moving their feet in order to help the alternate bouncing, tell them that when you say "change" they are to grab the ball with both hands as quickly as possible and do a quick turn about before continuing to bounce the ball in the opposite direction. If the movement is quick and strong the result will be a twisting action before the turning, to move in the opposite direction.

Part II: Movement Training

Request the children to find a space and listen. "Whenever I bang this drum or say *bang* you have to show me in mime or pantomime the part of your body that has been hit, either by clutching that part of you, or moving as you would if it were hit. Choose your own starting position, that is, kneeling or standing. Ready? 'Bang . . . Bang . . . ,' etc."

FIGURE 12.2

Suggest they choose a different part of themselves each time, that is, jaw, tummy, elbow, or shoulder. The next time, after showing where the "blow" has fallen, they should try sinking to the floor, rolling over and "dying." This is usually greeted with great glee and children will fall onto the ground without hurting themselves because they automatically twist and turn and then relax as they roll onto the floor. Allow a few more turns, then move directly to the apparatus part of the lesson. Since the latter requires a new arrangement of apparatus, leave plenty of time to organize this part of the lesson.

Part III: Apparatus Work

1. Cave: Arrange six ropes for six students to work together. Have the children stand a few feet away from the rope, then run, leap on to the rope and let their momentum carry them forward. They should turn at the highest point of their swing, then try to drop lightly onto the floor on the same spot that they started from. If they reach with their right hand higher up the rope than the left one, this will help turn the body to the left.

2. Four benches and two mats: (OR two benches inclined on two carpenters' sawhorses). This is a revision of "storming" but with a slight variation. Put the benches on opposite sides of the two supporting ones. Synchronize with a partner, run up the bench and turn in the air or show a twisted shape in the air, and land and roll. Pay special attention to stretching the feet in the air.

FIGURE 12.3

3. Bowling pins: Arranged in two lines with a variety of the size of spaces between the pins. Dribble a ball in and out of the spaces up one line, think of something different to do coming down the other.

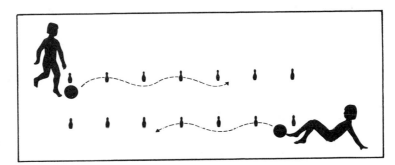

FIGURE 12.4

4. Box and springboard: Run and with a two-foot takeoff jump onto the box in an astride position. Reach about half-way up the box. The scissor vault is an easy one for all children to do involving a twist and a turn. Put the hands on the outer edges of the box. Lean forward and put all your weight on bent arms and at the same time swing your legs backward and upward. Cross one leg over the other side thus forcing the rest of the body to turn and the child can sit up facing the opposite direction.

FIGURE 12.5

5. Stage and mat: Run with a partner, jump on to the stage with a turn and go straight into a backward diagonal roll, on to feet again and walk along stage to stand opposite the mat. (Run, turn, in the air, land and roll.) Try to have the children work in twos and space themselves so there is constant activity without one pair pushing on the heels of the pair in

front. Aim for a tight curled backward roll and a strong stretched turning jump in the air finishing with a forward roll.

FIGURE 12.6

6. Large mat, chair, and an individual mat: Place the chair on its side, and ask the children (no more than two to a chair) to work out ways of performing rolls, and jumps showing a twist in the air. Individual mats can be placed over the chairs so that they can lie on them without hurting themselves.

FIGURE 12.7

7. Ropes: Climb a little way up the rope, transfer to the next rope, and show a twisted shape as you go. This could be from hanging for those whose arms are not strong or from an upside-down position.
8. Individual mats and wall or partners: Handstand or headstand against the wall, then twist from the waist as far as you can. Hold the position, then untwist, come down, and finish with a backward diagonal roll.

Lesson Reminder for Lesson No. 1

PART I: INTRODUCTORY ACTIVITY
    Free activity with balls followed by bouncing with quick turn.

PART II: MOVEMENT TRAINING
    Twisting and "dying."

PART III: APPARATUS WORK
1. Swing turn on ropes of Cave.
2. "Storming"—four benches.
3. Bowling pins.
4. "Scissors" on box.
5. Roll on—jump off stage.
6. Mat and chair and individual mat. Free choice.
7. Ropes—twisted shape.
8. Handstand sequence against wall.

DIAGRAM Q: Suggested Apparatus Arrangement for Lesson No. 1

Small mats	Section 2 4 benches and two mats		Section 3 Pins in two lines
	Section 5: Large mats	Section 4: Box	Section 1: Ropes in both bays of CAVE
	Section 7: Ropes	Section 6: Mat and chairs	Section 8: Wall

Lesson Nos. 2 and 3 (Twisting)

Part I: Introductory Activity

    Free play with balls followed by alternate hand bouncing. After some practice change to the following idea. "When I say 'change,' this time I want you to grab your ball, *turn* quickly around and throw it up in the air—catch it again and continue bouncing it as before." The children should aim at throwing it *accurately* in order to be able to reach up for it and keep control of it. Make sure that you move in an interesting zigzag pathway as you bounce your ball.

Part II: Movement Activity

Join up in twos. Work out a mock fight with your partner, where you first of all sustain a few blows then one or both "dies." There may be some classes where children would take advantage of this game to really hurt each other. The authors have never had this happen; we find boys in particular show much faithful television watching, with some wonderfully relaxed rolls on to the floor.

FIGURE 12.8

FIGURE 12.9

Part III: Apparatus Work

Same as previous lesson.

Lesson No. 4 (Twisting and Turning)

Part I: Introductory Activity

Hoops scattered at random. The children bounce or run and catch their ball moving between the hoops. They must not touch the hoops. Change direction and do something skillful with the ball.

The aim of this activity is to teach accurate and imaginative manipulation of the ball while forcing the children to move sensitively in and out of obstacles. The obstacles are the hoops and each other.

Part II: Movement Training

Begin with each child sitting inside a hoop. Present movement tasks such as, "Can you put three parts of yourself on the edge of the hoop?" "Can you put three parts on the hoop and make a twisted shape?"

FIGURE 12.10

FIGURE 12.11

Utility balls are useful in this area to enhance twisted shapes. Ask the children if they can make a twisted shape over the ball, then finish with a twisted shape holding the ball with some part of them.

Part III: Apparatus Work

A few ideas which may stimulate thought and interest are:

1. On the ropes: Three children who can climb could go up some distance and then come down with a "braiding" pattern. Children on the floor can keep the order right by having three skipping ropes in front of them and can call out when it is "one," "two," or "three's" turn to move.

FIGURE 12.12

2. Box: Encourage children on the Box to think of three separate movements. (Getting on, in the middle, getting off.) Limitations that stimulate new ideas might be to show a twist and a change of direction, or
show three different parts of yourself high, or make a group shape to
show variations in level and finish in different ways, but each way
with a twisting action.

Lesson Reminder for Lesson No. 4
PART I: INTRODUCTORY ACTIVITY
Bounce balls around hoops scattered on floor.

PART II: MOVEMENT TRAINING
Three parts on hoop.
Three parts and a twisted shape.

PART III: APPARATUS WORK
Same as previous lesson and/or apply ideas from previous section.

Lesson No. 5 (Twisting and Turning)

Part I: Introductory Activity
Running freely anywhere in the gymnasium. Next run in one-half of the
gymnasium and see if they can keep up their speed without bumping. Now
confine them to an even smaller area by using painted lines or making a
barrier with skipping ropes. Try moving slowly at first, twisting, and turning
to avoid each other, slowly gather speed. Finally, have a quick turn using
the whole gymnasium again!

Part II: Movement Training
Ask the children to find a space and lie on the floor on their backs. "Put
one leg over the other as far as you can while *keeping both* shoulders on the
floor. Try to feel a really strong twist in the waist as if you were a cloth
being 'wrung out.' What other position can you twist from?"

If ideas are slow in coming remember that the weight can be taken on
the shoulders, hands, feet, side, knees, or back. A small but attractive twist

FIGURE 12.13

FIGURE 12.14

can be experienced by the backward diagonal roll or from coming down from a handstand by putting both feet to the side.

Another attractive twisting action evolves when a child kneels with weight on hands and knees, then puts one hand as far as possible through the hole made by the other arm. If the hand is stretched enough the shoulder will reach the ground with a twisting action and the child can easily go into a sideways roll.

FIGURE 12.15

Part III: Apparatus Work

Same as previous lesson.

By this stage the children or you may have decided to alter apparatus arrangement or add further small apparatus. Some children are fond of skipping and may like to work out skipping patterns in twos or individually.

FIGURE 12.16

Those who do not have a vaulting box may balance two or three benches one on top of the other and if the children have had experience in using a springboard this can be combined with the benches.

A springboard may be used simply with a mat to get height for a twisted shape or a turn in the air—children like to jump through a hoop which can be held at an appropriate level for each child.

At the Cave, a flat bar high at the back of Bay 1, with a lower bar supporting the two saddles. At Bay 2 incline the ladder and put two narrow beams side by side at shoulder level. In both cases the children at this stage may be given a movement task requiring them to make up a sequence which shows a twist or a turn at some part of it.

Lesson Nos. 6 and 7 (Twisting and Turning)

Part I: Introductory Activity

Hoops in scattered formation. "Run in and out of the hoops and jump in quickly when I say 'change' and hold one of the twisted shapes of the previous lesson."

Part II: Movement Training

Make up a sequence with the class by inviting everyone to take a twisted shape, then you choose a shape and everyone does the same. All try a suitable movement of untwisting followed by a second twisted shape. All try, and repeat, or if the class has no problems, simply ask them to make up a sequence with a partner, on their own, or in a group of three. The twisting sequence could be given the added limitation of direction or level. An example of this might be to make their sequence go from low to high, or make their sequence involve moving away from their partner and returning again.

FIGURE 12.17

FIGURE 12.18

FIGURE 12.19

FIGURE 12.20

Part III: Apparatus Work

The following photograph of an idea for apparatus arrangement was thought out and organized by an individual group. Grade Four's idea with three benches piled one on top of the other and hoops on the very top did not work very well and was soon abandoned although a fair amount of thought and cooperative effort went into arranging it.

FIGURE 12.21   **FIGURE 12.22**

Grade Six tied a knot in two ropes and then suspended a bench from the stage to the ropes. By transferring from rope to rope they reached a second bench also inclined on two tied ropes but resting on the floor. This led to a final bench inclined on the basketball scaffolding.

The whole arrangement gave a great feeling of space, dimension, and a strong feeling of variation in levels.

When children invent their own arrangement of apparatus it is essential for them to have a limitation within which to work, otherwise much time can be wasted and a genuine challenge may be lacking. The limitation in the above apparatus work was to show a twisted shape somewhere, or twist and untwist as you move along up across and down.

Lesson No. 8 (Twisting and Turning)

Part I: Introductory Activity

Take a beanbag, balance it somewhere on your person, and move anywhere in the room. Put it between your heels and hop with it. Now jump
pulling your knees up quickly, and grab the beanbag with your hands. Try
again. Walk as quickly as you can with the beanbag on your head. Now
bend forward to throw the beanbag between your legs, turn quickly and
catch it.

FIGURE 12.23

FIGURE 12.24

Part II: Movement Training

Take a partner, sit on a mat beside her with the beanbag between your
feet.

FIGURE 12.25

1. Rock back slowly and put the beanbag in the hoop behind your heads and stretch out slowly.
2. Twist away from partner by keeping shoulders on the floor for as long as possible and lifting the leg nearest to your partner over your other leg.
3. Reach for your beanbag with the arm farthest away from your partner and put it between your shoulder blades.

FIGURE 12.26 **FIGURE 12.27** **FIGURE 12.28**

4. With a quick twist flick the beanbag off your back, then pick it up, put it between your feet, and sit up again.
5. Rock back once again, cross legs with your partner, and give her your beanbag while taking hers.

The above was a Grade Four sequence which has been described in detail to give you an idea of the type of sequence that can be developed with the use of small apparatus. This whole sequence was performed very slowly to insure maximum twisting and stretching, and to keep faithfully "in time" with the partner.

Part III: Apparatus Work
Same as previous lesson.

Lesson Reminder for Lesson No. 8
At this stage it is impossible to give lesson reminders for each teacher's arrangement of apparatus, even supposing it paralleled ours to start with must surely by now be individual and unique to her own class.

No two groups of children will develop an idea in exactly the same way. After the initial stages of experimentation, when children have experienced the wide challenge of a great variety of apparatus each calling for a totally different type of activity, it is *essential* to allow sufficient time for practice, repeating and repeating until a real feeling for form and fluency of movement is gained and quality emerges. This repetition may occur by staying at one piece of apparatus (after each group has experienced all) for several more lessons, or it may simply come about with time if you are lucky enough to have forty five-minute lessons.

Lesson No. 9 (Twisting and Turning)

Part I: Introductory Activity

Tell the children to run freely anywhere in the gymnasium and when you say "change," they join up with the nearest person and sit down. This is a way of getting children quickly into groups of various sizes. "This time I am going to call out a number and you must quickly join up in groups of that number and sit down—three—five—two—four—etc."

Part II: Movement Training

When you have the children sitting in groups of four explain the following "group game"—They stand up and join hands. When ready they must start to move, in, out, up, down and round but must never let go of hands and never stop moving until the teacher tells them to freeze. They must then balance in this shape whatever it is until you decide which is the best one. The others look at your choice and you explain why you like it, and off you go again.

FIGURE 12.29

FIGURE 12.30

FIGURE 12.31

Part III: Apparatus Work
Two ideas on the Southampton Cave.

| FIGURE 12.32 | FIGURE 12.33 | FIGURE 12.34 |

Lesson Nos. 10, 11 and 12 (Twisting with a Variation of Speed)

Part I: Introductory Activity
Ask the children to run *very quickly* then jump in the air, bend their knees fully on landing in order to go into a backward diagonal roll. They should come out of their roll *very slowly* and stand up. They should look for a space into which to run and repeat the movement with the main emphasis here in gathering speed for the strong push and turn and the contrasting deceleration of the roll.

Part II: Movement Training
Have the class make up a simple sequence which involves at least three twisting or turning movements, next ask them to do their sequence as fast as they can. Finally, do it in slow motion.

Ask them to decide which parts were easier to do fast and which ones were easier to do more slowly. "Now repeat the sequence varying the speed according to how you think it should be done."

If the children become absorbed in their sequence and very little time is left for apparatus work, do not hesitate to abandon the latter for this lesson. They can always do more of it next time.

In creating sequences one idea will spark off another and particularly in Grades Six and Seven, complicated patterns need time to be created and are often difficult to re-create if time is always cut short.

Part III: Apparatus Work
Same as previous lesson or continue above.

Qualities of Movement

We have shown in the Simon Fraser University film No. 5 the "Qualities of Movement, (see Appendix p. 210), as defined by Rudolf Laban whose analysis of movement underlies modern contemporary dance and has contributed significantly to the development of Movement Education. We have tried in this film to reassure our audience that quality in its generally understood sense is never lost from sight; it is encouraged in the gymnasium as it is in the art or music room, by every known teaching technique, but largely by an insistence that each child strives in every way to produce the best he is capable of.

Laban divided the elements in movement which refer to HOW a movement is performed into four separate classifications:

SPACE   FORCE   TIME   FLOW

Space in this classification refers to the flexible or direct use of space and has NOT been studied in our film series or approached in these introductory lessons.

Space, which we put into the category of *where* a movement can take place in terms of direction and level has already been discussed. In Parts Two and Three there are several lesson plans on space. We are, therefore, left with Force, Time, and Flow to consider.

Anyone who has stayed with us to this point need have no sudden alarm at facing three new concepts. You have been gradually discovering and your children have unconsciously been giving you endless examples of Force, Time, and Flow. Their *conscious* use is one which you can now develop as a further limitation giving added range, form, and thoughfulness to their work.

Force is simply the amount of strength required to perform a movement. At the end of this scale we have very strong forceful movements like leaping, pulling, and heaving and at the other end soft gentle movements such as stepping, rolling, or any movement requiring a minimum of strength.

Time refers to the speed with which a movement is performed, thus it can be accelerating, going very quickly, decelerating, or going very slowly.

Flow refers to the linking of one movement to the next in a natural and harmonious way, where each blends easily the one into the other. You must have many images in your mind from a simple jump, land and roll where the landing and rolling look like one single movement, to more complicated and successful sequences which the class has produced for you.

To show how inextricably the "qualities" of Force, Time, and Flow are often combined with each other, the above example of jump, land, and roll combine *Force* (strong muscular action to lift the body weight off the floor) and *Flow* landing and rolling. There are inevitable variations of the degrees of Force in landing and a deceleration of speed.

A theme or sub-theme of speed has just been illustrated in the previous lesson plan, where the children were asked to repeat their movements very quickly, then very slowly. They thus experienced a contrast which helped them to "feel" the quality more acutely.

Thus we have laid the foundations of Movement Education from which you can build. Your own understanding and appreciation of movement should be greatly enhanced and as a result your observations of the children.

Once you have made good use of boxes, canes, beanbags, hoops, benches (with hooks), wall bars, ropes, press for more sophisticated climbing apparatus. There are many listed in Appendix A and once installed can be used again and again by all the children *ad infinitum* (or until better equipment is yet designed). The art teacher insists on paints and supplies for craft works, the scientist clamours for more and more specialized equipment. We must do the same.

Chart to Show Intermediate Lesson Plans

S	Emphasis on Safety. Landing and Rolling	WHAT	*Establishing working atmosphere, leading into self-directed work stimulating imagination and cooperation within the group— standards of behavior to insure safety.*
A			
F		WHERE	
E	Adding Range, Bal. & Moving on Diff. Parts. Use of Partner	and	
T			
Y		HOW	

C	Stretching and Curling	WHAT	movement takes place
O			
N	Change of Direction	WHERE	movement takes place
T			
I			
N	Twisting and Turning	WHAT	with wider range of movements
U			
O			
U	Force Time Flow	HOW	the movement takes place. *Beginning to combine two movement factors consciously. Sequence building teaches flow, which, in turn, builds upon widening movement vocabulary.*
S			

Possible Developments

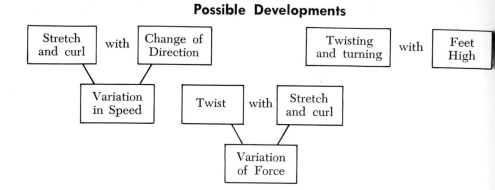

Appendixes

Appendix A: Instructional Aids and Human Resources
Appendix B: Apparatus, Equipment, and Supplies
Appendix C: Definition of Terms Used in Movement Education
Appendix D: Apparatus, Equipment, and Supply Companies

Part Four is a resource file of appropriate audiovisual aids, written materials and recommended apparatus and equipment for Movement Education programs. Appendix A contains an annotated list of Movement Education films, a summary of current text books on this subject, and a list of experts in this field who are available for conferences, workshops, and short term appointments. Appendix B includes diagrams and descriptions of commercial and inexpensive apparatus recommended for use in elementary school programs. Appendix C includes a glossary of terms used in Movement Education. Finally Appendix D contains the names and addresses of manufacturers and suppliers of equipment and agility apparatus.

APPENDIX A

Instructional Aids and Human Resources

Visual Aids

Human Resources

Written Materials

There is a growing source of outstanding technical and human resources available on the subject of Movement Education. So often, however, this information is rarely made known to supervisors of physical education or classroom teachers. Appendix A provides a summary list of written, visual and human resources currently available on this subject.

Although the resources listed are far from complete, they will provide an adequate supplement to any interested teacher. Since the Movement Education approach is difficult to describe in writing, films become extremely important to college teachers and consultants in illustrating the organizational structure and methods of instruction of this approach to teaching physical education. Similarly, the Movement Education specialists listed under "Human Resources" can provide invaluable assistance in such areas as consulting services, conference workshops, and short-term appointments to universities and school districts. All written materials may be obtained by writing directly to the publisher or through local book distributors.

Visual Aids

The accompanying list of films have been previewed by the writers and/or recommended by leading experts in the field. Wherever possible, we have listed the price and other facts relating to preview fees and geographical rental restrictions.

Simon Fraser University's Film Series

Simon Fraser University's Film Series contain five instructional films on Movement Education which are specifically designed to be used by classroom teachers and for teacher training programs. The films in this series were taken under normal teaching conditions in a typical elementary school in British Columbia, Canada. Children ranging in age from five to thirteen were filmed at sequential periods over a period of one school year. Film sequences were selected from over twenty thousand feet of film and illustrate basic elements, creative uses of equipment and apparatus, and numerous examples of various methods and techniques used in this approach. This series may, therefore, be considered a complementary visual supplement to each chapter in this book or to any available text which describes the Movement Education approach.

The following five films may be purchased from the Audio-Visual Centre, Simon Fraser University, Burnaby 2, British Columbia, Canada. Delivery time is normally ten days. Purchase and rental prices are listed under each film.

Film No. 1: Introduction to Movement Education (16 mm., 36 minutes, sound, color)

Film No. 1 is designed to give classroom teachers, with no prior knowledge of Movement Education, a general overview of the content and methods that are used in this approach to teaching physical activities. In the initial sequences, the philosophy underlying this approach is presented to show the compatibility of Movement Education with the modern concept of education. This is followed by a description of the three basic elements of Movement Education and how they are taught. Strong emphasis is given to the limitation and indirect methods of instruction in this and all remaining films of this series. Special attention is also given to "safety training," a procedure which must be understood and emphasized in every lesson utilizing this approach. Since this is an introductory film we have attempted to show a wide variety of small and large apparatus used in typical lessons throughout this project. Continuous reference is made in this film to more elaborate coverages of key aspects of Movement Education in the remaining four films.

Purchase Price: $250.00

Rental: $30.00 first day; $10.00 each succeeding day.

Film No. 2: Developing Range and Understanding of Movement (16 mm., 29 minutes, sound, color)

This film describes one of the primary elements of Movement Education most commonly defined as "Body Awareness." It illustrates how children learn to control and manipulate the weight of the body on the floor, with small equipment and with large apparatus. Several sequences show children of various ages using agility or climbing apparatus.

A major emphasis of this film has been to illustrate movement tasks requiring children to move and balance on different parts of the body, to work with a partner and within a group and to develop specific themes of stretch, curl, and twist. Excerpts of a lesson plan entitled "feet high" is also included to show how two parts of a lesson complement each other.

Purchase Price: $210.00.

Rental: $25.00 first day; $10.00 each succeeding day.

Film No. 3: Understanding Space and Directional Movements (16 mm., 26 minutes, sound, color)

This film illustrates how teachers can assist children to develop a conceptual understanding and an effective use of general and limited space. It shows how to gradually expand a child's movement vocabulary to include such directional movements as forward, sideways, across, around, and through.

The first part of the film attempts to lay the groundwork for this important aspect of Movement Education. Children are shown in their initial lessons developing the full use of all available space on or off apparatus. Several scenes clearly illustrate how children develop spatial awareness as well as an awareness of the safety of themselves and other members of the class. A lesson plan emphasizing the use of general and limited space is also provided as a guideline for beginning teachers. Numerous illustrations of constructive and creative use of equipment and apparatus have been included to show how children, when given the opportunity, can become the initiators of their own learning experiences.

Purchase Price: $200.00

Rental: $25.00 first day; $10.00 each succeeding day.

Film No. 4: How to Develop a Theme (16 mm., 31 minutes, sound, color)

The primary purpose of this film is to show, in a sequential pattern, how Movement Education is taught through a series of themes. Although a theme is similar to the contemporary "instructional unit," it has a uniqueness of its own and needs general clarification. Hence, the film illustrates how a theme is first introduced to a variety of age levels and how it is developed in progressive stages.

One of the most interesting aspects of this film is the "before and after" visual demonstration showing a general improvement in a child's ability to draw upon an increased movement vocabulary. The themes of "stretch and curl" and "twisting" are illustrated both at primary and intermediate levels to show contrast in abilities, particularly in the use of small equipment and large apparatus.

Purchase Price: $230.00

Rental: $30.00 first day; $10.00 each succeeding day.

Film No. 5: Qualities of Movement (16 mm., 27 minutes, sound, color)

This film describes what Rudolp Laban defined as the qualities of movement. A distinction is first drawn between the terms "quality," as it is generally understood in gymnastics and other sports, and "qualities" of movement, as defined by the originator of Movement Education.

In the remaining portion of the film, the qualities of "force," "time," and "flow" are illustrated by a variety of age levels. A theme combining all three qualities is included to show how each quality can be integrated into one theme. For interest and comparison, a sequence performed by a group of university students has been included in the latter part of the film.

Purchase Price: $200.00

Rental: $25.00 first day; $10.00 each succeeding day.

Individual Films

Title: Children in Action

Details: 16 mm., color, sound, 24 minutes.

Distributor: Divisional Education Offices, Education Offices, Market Street, Nelson, Lancaster, England.

DESCRIPTION:

This film was directed by Percy Jones (co-author of *Physical Education in the Primary Schools*) and shows upper elementary school-age children participating in various aspects of a movement education lesson. There are excellent illustrations of individual and partner sequences. Apparatus arrangement is also worth special notation. The presentation of movement tasks as well as methods of increasing the challenges on the floor and apparatus has been exceptionally well illustrated.

Title: Movement Education in the Primary School

Details: 16 mm., color, sound, 26 minutes.

Distributor: Somerset County Film Library, Mount Street, Bridgwater, Somerset, England.

DESCRIPTION:

The basic elements of Space, Weight, and Time are illustrated in this film. Children ranging in age from seven to eleven are shown developing movement skills during the movement training and apparatus part of the lesson. The concepts of space, weight, and time are closely described and illustrated. Teachers will find many ideas relating to technique and the creative use of apparatus throughout this film.

Title: Junior School Physical Education Lesson

Details: 16 mm., color, sound, 25 minutes.

Distributor: County Film Library, 2 Walton's Parade, Preston, Lancashire, England.

DESCRIPTION:

This film shows a typical English junior-level group of students in a physical education lesson. The children have been given instruction prior to going into the recreation area. They demonstrate the use of various apparatus, how to work alone, in pairs, and in groups. The teacher's role is shown as a guide to the activities.

Title: I. M. March College Gymnastic Film
Details: 16 mm., black and white, sound, 20 minutes.
Distributor: I. M. March College, Liverpool, England.

DESCRIPTION:

Senior women's physical education specialists demonstrate "limbering" as preparation for a gymnastic lesson. This is followed by students working in pairs on specific movement tasks. Vaulting and agility problems are set in connection with the different pieces of apparatus.

Title: Educational Gymnastics—Secondary Girls, 4th Year
Details: 16 mm., black and white, sound, 2 reels: 24 minutes.
Distributor: Foundation Film Library, Brooklands House, Weybridge, Surrey.

DESCRIPTION:

This is a teaching film for girls showing a variety of movement qualities and techniques. More background classwork would have added interest but the teaching points of the individual sequences were well illustrated. The commentary could have given a clearer indication of the tasks to the groups.

Title: And So The Move
Details: 16 mm., black and white, sound, 20 minutes.
Distributor: Audio-Visual Center, Michigan State University, East Lansing, Michigan.

DESCRIPTION:

This is a film showing the application of movement education to physically handicapped elementary school children. Numerous practical and meaningful activities in fundamental movement experiences are presented with accompanying theoretical narration on the value of the activities. Suggestions are included for sequence in programming based on a problem-solving approach.

Title: Basic Movement Education in England
Details: 16 mm., black and white, sound, 19 minutes.
Purchase Price: $85.00, Rental: $4.25
Distributor: Audio-Visual Education Center, University of Michigan, 720 East Huron Street, Ann Arbor, Michigan.

DESCRIPTION:

This film describes movement education from primary grades through teaching training in England. The use of small and large apparatus is shown in a variety of interesting situations. The film demonstrates how to bring a child to an awareness of his relationship to space, time, and force.

Title: Movement Experiences for Children
Details: 16 mm., black and white, sound, 7 minutes.
Distributor: Department of Instructional Media Distribution, Altgeld 114, Northern Illinois University, DeKalb, Illinois.

DESCRIPTION:

A short documentary film on the need for children to move and to learn to move well which includes delightful pictures of children in natural outdoor activities followed by a view of an experimental indoor program using a problem-solving approach.

Title: Movement Experiences for Primary Children
Details: 16 mm., color, sound, 17 minutes.
Distributor: Department of Instructional Media Distribution, Altgeld 114, Northern Illinois University, DeKalb, Illinois.

DESCRIPTION:

This film includes a comprehensive coverage of how ideas of movement education are taught to elementary school children. Children are shown developing movement ideas on the floor and later on a wide variety of apparatus and new agility equipment. Emphasis is given to appropriate teaching methods used in movement education.

Title: Movement Education in Physical Education
Details: 16 mm., black and white, sound, 20 minutes.
Purchase Price: $145.00; Rental: $25.00
Distributor: Hayes Kruger, Louise Duffy School, 95 Westminster Drive, West Hartford, Connecticut.

DESCRIPTION:

This film interprets movement education through narration in question-answer form. Two teachers from the program provide much information on a variety of activities from K-6. The film demonstrates the methodology of the problem-solving approach, emphasizes the importance of a well-structured environment, and discusses the relationship to good traditional programming.

Title: Movement Exploration
Details: 16 mm., color, sound, 20 minutes.
Purchase Price: $185.00, Rental: $20.00 first day; $10.00 each additional day.
Distributor: Documentary Films, 3217 Trout Gulch Road, Aptos, California.

DESCRIPTION:

This film is designed for K-6 teachers and teachers-in-training. The film includes a wide range of activities involving primary and elementary children, such as: locomotor skills, ball handling, hoops, jump ropes, apparatus and improvised equipment. Emphasis is on involvement of each child for maximum participation with a problem-solving approach. It shows relationship to fitness and preparation for well-known adult sports activities.

Title: Movement Education in Physical Education
Details: 16 mm., black and white, sound, 17 minutes.
Purchase Price: $50.00, Rental: $3.00
Distributor: The Audio-Visual Center, Division and Extension and University Services, University of Iowa, Iowa City, Iowa. (Films not available for rental or preview outside U.S.A.)

DESCRIPTION:

In this film, emphasis is placed on present movement patterns based on skills for daily work and play activities to children in the first grade and the relationship of these patterns to their activities throughout the elementary grades.

Title: Time and Space Awareness
Details: 16 mm., black and white, sound, 8 minutes.
Purchase Price: $25.00, Rental: $1.65
Distributor: The Audio-Visual Center, Division and Extension and University Services, University of Iowa, Iowa City, Iowa. (Films not available for rental or preview outside U.S.A.)

DESCRIPTION:

This film illustrates a sample lesson emphasizing time and space, two of the components of movement which are then transferred to a game situation.

Title: Movement Education—Guided Exploration
Details: 16 mm., black and white, sound, 8 minutes.
Purchase Price: $25.00, Rental $1.65
Distributor: The Audio-Visual Center, Division and Extension and University Services, University of Iowa, Iowa City, Iowa. (Films not available for rental or preview outside U.S.A.)

DESCRIPTION:

The teaching techniques used as children explore with hoops, jump ropes, and balls are highlighted in this demonstration film.

Title: Movement Education—The Problem-Solving Technique
Details: 16 mm., black and white, sound, 12 minutes.
Purchase Price: $30.00, Rental $1.65
Distributor: The Audio-Visual Center, Division and Extension and University
                    Services, University of Iowa, Iowa City, Iowa. (Films not avail-
                    able for rental or preview outside U.S.A.)

DESCRIPTION:

This film demonstrates keen fifth graders developing a dance using simple folk steps and music. The emphasis is on the teaching technique of problem-solving, rather than on the finished dance product.

Title: Educational Gymnastics in England—From Primary to College Level
         Programs.
Details: 16 mm., color, sound, 30 minutes.
Purchase Price: $240, Rental $30.00 first day, $10.00 each succeeding day.
Distributor: Audio-Visual Centre, Simon Fraser University, Burnaby 2, B. C.,
                    Canada.

DESCRIPTION:

This film is a visual documentation of Dr. Kirchner's observations of educational gymnastic programs in England (1969). The film illustrates the role and emphasis of educational gymnastics in elementary, high school, and college programs. In the majority of scenes, typical programs are shown to illustrate the methods used, levels of performance and differences in facilities and equipment. The film also shows a few advanced educational gymnastic programs to illustrate the quality of performance that can be reached through this type of program.

Human Resources

The following list of specialists in the area of Movement Education are among the many currently teaching in Canada or in the United States. Each person listed is available for speaking engagements, workshops, or possible short term appointments. For information relating to consulting fees, available times, etc., write directly to the specialist.

Since there are so many well qualified specialists in England, both at the college level and within each school district, we have not singled out a partial list. Central directories are provided and can be of tremendous assistance in providing names of qualified teachers and college personnel in this area.

Miss Naomi Allenhaugh

Present position: Professor, Department of Physical Education,
                    Ohio State University, Columbus, Ohio.

Background: Author, teacher (U.S.A.), teacher training and experimental
                    programs in Movement Education.

Miss Kate R. Barrett

Present position: Physical Education Specialist, Campus School, The University of Wisconsin, Milwaukee, Wisconsin.

Background: Author, teacher (England and U.S.A.), experimental programs in Movement Education.

Miss Nora Chatwin

Present position: Program Consultant, (P.E.) Ontario, Department of Education, East Central Region, 29 Gervais Drive, Don Mills, Ontario, Canada.

Background: Author, teacher (Canada and England), experimental programs in Movement Education.

Dr. Shirley Howard Cooper

Present position: Professor, Department of Physical Education for Women, University of Michigan, Ann Arbor, Michigan.

Background: Author, teacher (U.S.A.), teacher training and experimental programs in Movement Education.

Mrs. Jean Cunningham

Present position: Associate, Department of Physical Development Studies, Simon Fraser University, Burnaby 2, British Columbia, Canada.

Background: Author, teacher (Canada, Jamaica, England), teacher training supervisor, experimental programs in Movement Education.

Miss Margaret Ellis

Present position: Assistant Professor, Faculty of Education, University of Alberta, Edmonton, Alberta, Canada.

Background: Teacher (Canada and England), teacher training supervisor, experimental programs in Movement Education.

Dr. Bette Jean Logsdon

Present position: Professor, Department of Physical Education, Ohio State University, Columbus, Ohio.

Background: Author, teacher (U.S.A.), teacher training and experimental programs in Movement Education.

Dr. Glenn Kirchner

Present position: Professor and Head, Department of Physical Development Studies, Simon Fraser University, Burnaby 2, British Columbia, Canada.

Background: Author, teacher (Canada, U.S.A.), teacher training and experimental programs in Movement Education.

Mr. Hayes Kruger

Present position: Teacher, Louis Duffy Elementary School, West Hartford, Connecticut.

Background: Author, teacher (U.S.A.), experimental programs in Movement Education.

Dr. Lorena Porter

Present position: Professor, Department of Physical Education for Women, Northern Illinois University, DeKalb, Illinois.

Background: Author, teacher (U.S.A.), teacher training and experimental programs in Movement Education.

Miss Valerie A. Proyer

Present position: Assistant Professor, MacDonald College of McGill University, Ste Anne De Bellevue, Quebec, Canada.

Background: Author, teacher (Canada and England), teacher training, experimental programs in Movement Education.

Miss Lois Pye

Present position: Assistant Professor, Department of Physical Education for Women, Oregon State College, Corvallis, Oregon.

Background: Author, Teacher (England and U.S.A.), teacher training supervisor, experimental programs in Movement Education.

Mr. Stuart G. Robbins

Present position: Assistant Professor, Faculty of Education, University of Alberta, Edmonton, Alberta, Canada.

Background: Teacher (Canada and England), supervisor of teacher training programs. experimental programs in Movement Education.

Miss Patricia W. Tanner

Present position: Doctoral candidate, Ohio State University, Columbus, Ohio.

Background: Author, teacher (England and U.S.A.), experimental programs in Movement Education.

Mrs. Joan Tillotson

Present position: Project Director, Program of Movement Education for Plattsburgh Elementary Schools, Plattsburgh, New York.

Background: Author, Teacher (U.S.A.), supervisor, experimental programs in Movement Education.

Miss Eileen Warrell

Present position: Assistant Professor, Department of Physical Development Studies, Simon Fraser University, Burnaby 2, British Columbia, Canada.

Background: Author, teacher (Canada, Jamaica, England), teacher training supervisor, experimental programs in Movement Education.

Mrs. Jane Young

Present position: Elementary Physical Education Specialist, Middletown Schools, Middletown, Ohio.

Background: Teacher (England and U.S.A.), experimental programs in Movement Education.

Central Directories

The following associations may be contacted regarding names and addresses of Movement Education experts. As a suggestion, indicate the type of qualifications required for the position. Information relating to workshops, conference speaker, or short term appointment, will assist in finding the right person.

1. British Association of Organizers and Lecturers in Physical Education.
2. The Physical Education Association of Great Britain and Northern Ireland, Ling House, 10, Nottingham Place, London W. 1., England.
3. The Canadian Association for Health, Physical Education and Recreation, Toronto, Canada.
4. The American Association for Health, Physical Education and Recreation, 1201 16th Street, N. W., Washington, D. C., U. S. A.

Written Materials

Written materials on Movement Education are listed under a variety of topics. Several authors use terms such as "educational gymnastics," "movement exploration," "movement training," or "basic movement," to describe this approach to teaching physical education. Generally speaking, they are similar to Movement Education in meaning, content, and methods of instructions advocated.

The following list of basic references should assist the reader in selecting supplementary references for his personal library.

General References on Content and Methodology*

BILBROUGH, A., AND JONES, P., *Physical Education in the Primary School*, London: University of London Press, Ltd., 1964. 176 pages.

BROWN, M. C. and SOMMERS, B. K. *Movement Education; its Evolution and a Modern Approach*, Reading, Mass.: Addison-Wesley Publishing Co., 1969.

CAMERON, W., AND PLEASANCE, P., *Education in Movement*, Oxford: Basil Blackwell and Mott, Ltd., 1963, 56 pages.

COPE, J., *Discovery Methods in Physical Education*, London: Thomas Nelson and Sons, Ltd., 1967.

HACKETT, L. C., AND JANSON, R. G., *A Guide to Movement Exploration*, Peak Publications, 982 El Cajon Way, Palo Alto, California, 74 pages.

HALSEY, E., AND PORTER, L., *Physical Education for Children*, Revised Edition, New York: Holt, Rinehart & Winston, Inc., 1967, 449 pages.

GRAY, V., AND PERCIVAL, R. *Music, Movement and Mime for Children*, London: Oxford Press, 1966, 110 pages.

JORDAN, D., *Childhood and Movement*, Oxford: Basil Blackwell & Mott, Ltd., 1966.

JOYNSON, D. C., *Physical Education for Children*, 3rd Edition, London: Kaye and Ward, Ltd., 1967.

KIRCHNER, G., *Physical Education for Elementary School Children*, Second Edition. Dubuque: Wm. C. Brown Company Publishers, 1970.

LABAN, R., Second Edition Revised by Lisa Ullman, *Modern Educational Dance*, London: MacDonald & Evans, Ltd., 1963, 114 pages.

London County Council, *Educational Gymnastics*, London: London Education Authority, 1964, 60 pages.

London County Council, *Movement Education for Infants*, London: London Education Authority, 1966, 63 pages.

MAULDON, E., AND LAYDON, L., *Teaching Gymnastics*, London: MacDonald & Evans, Ltd., 1965, 192 pages.

Ministry of Education, *Moving and Growing*, London: Her Majesty's Stationery Office, 1953, 68 pages.

Ministry of Education, *Planning the Program*, London: Her Majesty's Stationery Office, 1953, 72 pages.

MORISON, R., *A Movement Approach to Educational Gymnastics*, London: J. M. Dent and Sons, Ltd., 1969.

NORTH, M., *A Simple Guide to Movement Teaching*, Exeter: A. Wheaton & Co., Ltd., 1964, 87 pages.

————, *Composing Movement Sequences*, Exeter: A. Wheaton & Co., Ltd., 1965.

PALLETT, D. G., *Modern Educational Gymnastics*, New York: Pergamon Press, Inc., 1965, 128 pages.

RANDALL, M., *Basic Movement*, London: G. Bell and Sons, Ltd., 1963, 105 pages.

RUSSELL, J., *Modern Dance in Education*, London: MacDonald & Evans, Ltd., 1958, 99 pages.

————, *Creative Dance in the Primary School*, London: MacDonald & Evans, Ltd., 1965, 68 pages.

---

*For convenience all books printed in England may be purchased from the Ling Book Shop, 10, Nottingham Place, London W. 1. England.

SHURR, E. L., *Movement Experiences for Children,* New York: Appleton-Century-Crofts, 1966.

WILLES, A. W. *Small Apparatus for Primary School Physical Education,* Melbourne: The University Bookroom, University of Melbourne, Australia, 1965, 136 pages.

History and Theoretical Bases of Movement Education

LABAN, R., Second Edition revised and enlarged by Lisa Ullmann, *The Mastery of Movement,* London: MacDonald & Evans, Ltd., 1960, 186 pages.

————, *Choreutics,* London: MacDonald & Evans, Ltd., 1966, 214 pages.

LABAN, R., AND LAWRENCE, F. C., *Effort,* London: MacDonald & Evans, Ltd., 1947, 88 pages.

REDFERN, B., Introducing *Laban Art of Movement,* London: MacDonald & Evans, Ltd., 1965, 32 pages.

APPENDIX B

Apparatus, Equipment, and Supplies

Small Apparatus
Large Apparatus
Agility or Climbing Apparatus

In the previous chapters numerous suggestions have been made with respect to the use of small and large apparatus in Movement Education lessons. Several items, such as beanbags, hoops, and vaulting boxes are quite familiar to classroom teachers. Other apparatus, however, such as individual mats and the new types of Agility Apparatus are new to the majority of elementary school teachers. Information pertaining to cost, number required, plans for construction, and suggestions relating to the care and maintenance of all apparatus is provided in this Appendix.

Since the majority of the equipment used in gymnastics with a Movement Education approach is classified as "Small Apparatus," we have given this a separate coverage. The next section, Large Apparatus, covers the basic heavy apparatus which may be purchased from most local athletic supply companies. We recognize the limitations of most school budgets and have provided plans for the construction of a few of the more important apparatus. The last section entitled Agility or Climbing Apparatus includes a reasonable coverage of the most widely used Agility Apparatus. The latter equipment is extremely important to the apparatus section of each movement lesson. The authors, as well as virtually all leading experts in this field, cannot overemphasize the importance of this apparatus.

Small Apparatus

The basic use of the following equipment should be to increase the skill of a specific movement and to stimulate an individual's exploration of the movement idea. Small apparatus, if used creatively, will provide an additional dimension to every movement task.[1] Several items, such as the individual mats, hoops, and canes are also used in conjunction with the large apparatus for the same reasons.

In terms of priorities, it is strongly recommended the following small apparatus be purchased:

Individual mats	Canes
Utility balls	Blocks
Hoops	Pins, no cost (used bowling pins)
Beanbags	Rubber bands, no cost
Skipping ropes	Cloth braids

Individual Mats

Size 18" x 36" x ¾" to 1" Number 40 (one per child)
Material: rubber or synthetic
Price: Range from $3.00 to $5.00

Distributor:
    Canada: George Sparlings Ltd.,
              929 Grandville Street
              Vancouver 6, British Columbia, Canada.
              Jaffary's Athletic Equipment,
              165 West 6th Avenue,
              Vancouver, British Columbia, Canada.

FIGURE B1

Care and Maintenance
1. Establish one place in the storage room where mats are to be permanently stored. A dolly on four castors is the easiest method of storing and moving mats (see Diagram R).

2. Teach children to carry mats with both hands, holding the long side. Do not allow children to drag, throw, or kick mats.

3. Mark one side of each mat (India ink) and insist this side is always facing up.

4. Teach children to put mats away in pairs. Clean sides always facing each other.

---

[1] A. W. Willee, *Small Apparatus for Primary School Physical Education,* Melbourne: the University Bookroom, University of Melbourne, Australia, 1965.

DIAGRAM R: Mat Storage Dolly

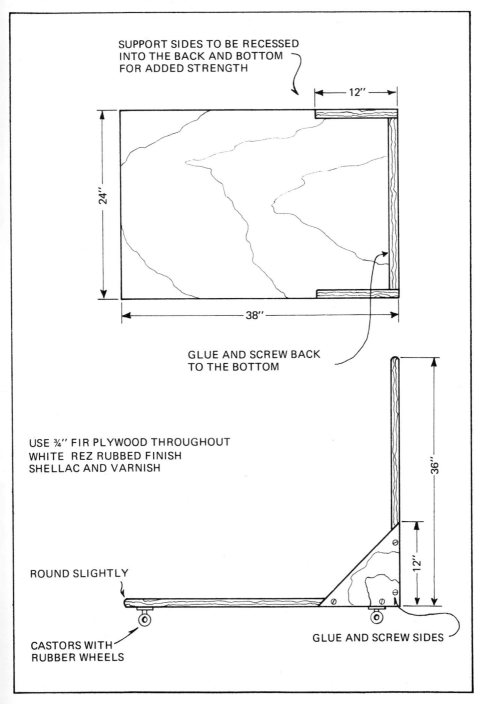

SUPPORT SIDES TO BE RECESSED
INTO THE BACK AND BOTTOM
FOR ADDED STRENGTH

12"

24"

38"

GLUE AND SCREW BACK
TO THE BOTTOM

USE ¾" FIR PLYWOOD THROUGHOUT
WHITE REZ RUBBED FINISH
SHELLAC AND VARNISH

36"

12"

ROUND SLIGHTLY

CASTORS WITH
RUBBER WHEELS

GLUE AND SCREW SIDES

FIGURE B2

Hoops
Size: Range 24″, 30″, and 36″
Number: 40 (one per child)
Material: Wood or plastic
Price: Range from $1.00 to
$2.00
Distributor: Local athletic
supply company

FIGURE B3

Beanbags
Size: 4″ x 6″
Number: 40 (one per child)
Material: Cloth cover, beans
Price: 25 cents to 40 cents
Distributor: Local athletic
supply company

FIGURE B4

Ropes
Size: Long ropes 5/8″ x 13′,
14′ and 15′
short ropes 5/8″ x 6′, 7′,
8′, 9′
Number: 2 of each size in
long ropes
10 of each size in
short ropes

Material: Sash, nylon, or plastic
Price: Depends on material. Buy long rope and cut as suggested below:

To Cut Ropes
1. Measure off the desired length of rope.
2. Wrap five inches above and below the cut mark with tape (plastic pre-
    ferred; adhesive acceptable).
3. Place rope on small wooden block and cut rope in middle of taped area.

To Mark Ropes
   Since there may be three or four different lengths of rope, dip the ends
of the ropes in different colored paint to represent short, medium, and long
lengths. (Dip about six inches.)

DIAGRAM S: Skipping Ropes

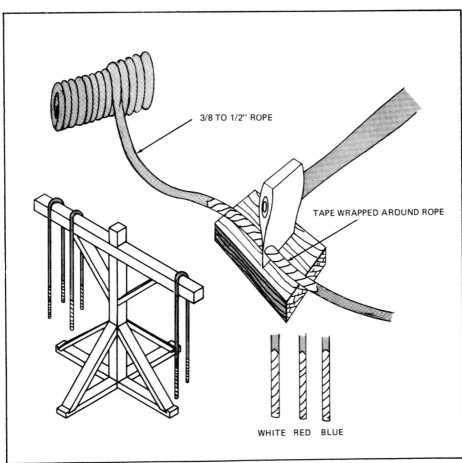

3/8 TO 1/2″ ROPE

TAPE WRAPPED AROUND ROPE

WHITE   RED   BLUE

FIGURE B5

Canes
Size: 6 feet to 7 feet
Number: 15 to 20
Material: Thin bamboo or dowling
Price: 50 cents to $1.00 each
Distributor: Local lumber company and rug firms (bamboo is sometimes used to roll carpet).

Blocks
Size: 24 of 12″ x 4″ x 4″
      12 of 24″ x 4″ x 4″
Number: 40
Material: Standard 4″ x 4″ fir lumber stock
Price: Depends on local area
Distributor: Local lumber company

DIAGRAM T: How to Construct Wooden Blocks

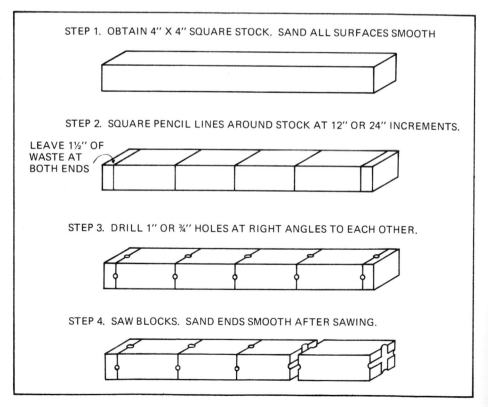

STEP 1. OBTAIN 4″ X 4″ SQUARE STOCK. SAND ALL SURFACES SMOOTH

STEP 2. SQUARE PENCIL LINES AROUND STOCK AT 12″ OR 24″ INCREMENTS.

LEAVE 1½″ OF WASTE AT BOTH ENDS

STEP 3. DRILL 1″ OR ¾″ HOLES AT RIGHT ANGLES TO EACH OTHER.

STEP 4. SAW BLOCKS. SAND ENDS SMOOTH AFTER SAWING.

Utility Balls
Size: 6" x 24"
Number: 40 (one per child)
Material: All types of balls (soccer, basketball, tennis, etc., are acceptable)
Price: Depends upon size and quality of ball
Distributor: Local athletic supply company

FIGURE B6

Bowling Pins
Size: 12" to 20"
Number: 16 to 20
Material: Wood or plastic
Price: Depends on material (see suggestion)
    Construction of "homemade" pin—ask local bowling alley for "used" ten-pins. Modify as suggested below.  cut off top inch.

Rubber Bands
Size: 1½" bands
Number: 40 (one for each child)
Material: Rubber
Price: See below

FIGURE B7

Construction of Homemade Bands
    The best type of inner tube is one used in tractor size tires. However, the inner tubes used in most automobile tires are quite suitable. With ordinary scissors, cut across the tube, then cut three or four bands. At the end of the fourth cut you will have an undesirable angle; cut this piece (see diagram) off and begin the next series of cuts. After cutting the bands, wash

them with regular soap and water to remove dirt and powder usually found on the inside of the tube. For efficient storage, tie a rope around the bands and hang them in your storage room.

DIAGRAM U: Inner Tube Tires

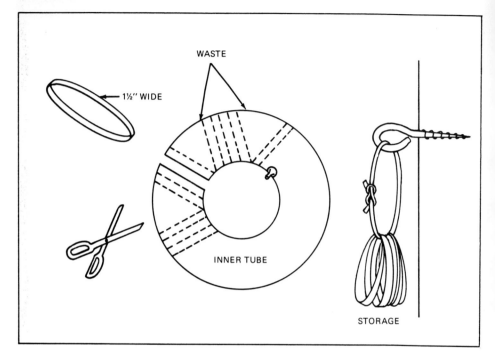

Large Apparatus

Large apparatus, which also includes all Agility Equipment described in the next section, are used during the second part of a Movement Education lesson. This section, however, will cover apparatus which may be in the majority of elementary schools and with which most teachers are reasonably familiar.

With respect to the importance to the program, it is recommended the following be purchased or constructed:

Balance bench	Springboard
Vaulting box	Sawhorse
Climbing ropes	Optional equipment
Large mats	

The writers do not recommend the use of a trampoline or trampet in a Movement Education program.

Balance Bench

Size: 12″ high x 8 feet long with reversible use (top side 10″, bottom 2½″)
Distributor: Athletic supplies companies (see Appendix D)
Basic features: See specifications below:

FIGURE B8

DIAGRAM V: How to Construct a Balance Bench

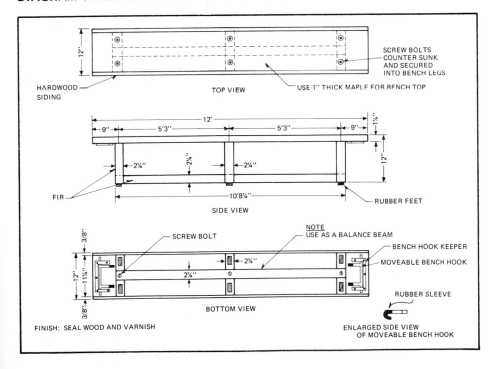

Vaulting Box

Size: 4 feet wide x 4 feet 6" high
Distributor: Athletic supply companies (see Appendix D)
Price range: $100.00 to $250.00
Basic features: See specifications below:

DIAGRAM W: Suggested Plans for a Vaulting Box

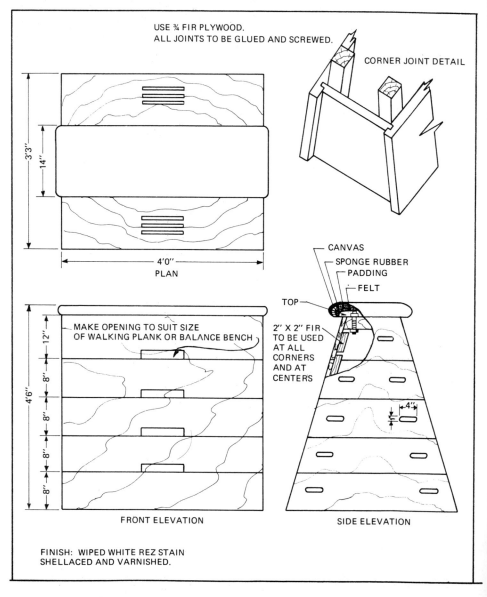

Climbing Ropes
Size: Length depends on ceiling height, thickness 2″ diameter
Distributor: Athletic supply companies (see Appendix D)
Basic features: European hemp or synthetic ropes are both recommended. In multiples of two or more, allow two feet between each rope.

FIGURE B9

Large Mats
Size: 4 feet x 6 feet
Distributor: Athletic supply companies (see Appendix D)
Basic features: Recommend light-weight synthetic mats with covers and carrying straps, or hole along sides.

Springboard
Size: Standard equipment
Distributor: Athletic supply companies (see Appendix D)
Basic features: Standard equipment

Sawhorse
Size: as diagram
Distributor: Homemade—see diagram
Basic features: see diagram

Wall Bars
Size: Standard equipment
Distributor: Athletic supply companies (see Appendix D)
Basic features: Standard equipment

DIAGRAM X: Sawhorse

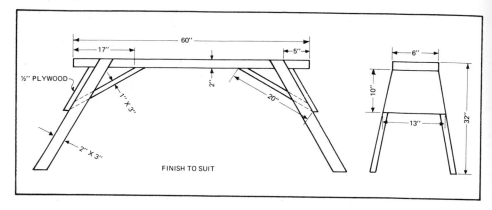

Agility or Climbing Apparatus

Agility or climbing apparatus are as important to Movement Education as books are to academic subjects. This equipment, if creatively used by the teacher and class, provide an immense challenge and enrichment of all movement experiences. Movement ideas that have been tried during the movement training part of the lesson should be applied to challenging apparatus. Vaulting boxes and balance benches certainly present a challenge but not nearly as great as the apparatus found in this section.

Teachers who are hesitant to use the following apparatus are reminded that no child will attempt a movement task on any piece of equipment until he is physically and mentally ready. Furthermore, each child is taught to progress at his own rate, hence, the element of competition is a personal rather than a group factor. Finally, and a reassuring point, the number of accidents on this type of apparatus in Movement Education programs is significantly fewer than in contemporary physical education programs.

The following agility apparatus is not listed according to the writers' personal preferences. Each type of equipment has certain special advantages as well as several basic limitations. Accordingly, basic information relating to cost, space requirements, and unique features is listed under each type of apparatus.

J. E. G. Equipment (indoor-outdoor)

Type: Portable.

Space requirements: Adaptable to any area.

Storage requirements: Minimum requirements—3 feet x 5 feet.

Price range: American $800.00—$900.00 full set
            Canadian $800.00—$900.00 full set

FIGURE B10

Basic Features
1. Welded structural steel tubing.
2. May be used in gymnasium, classroom, or hallway, plus out-of-doors.
3. Multiple arrangements of apparatus.
4. Can be moved and assembled by primary children.
Distributor:
> Educational Consultants Ltd.
> 1393 Greenbriar Way
> North Vancouver, B. C. Canada

Cave—Southampton (indoor)

Type: Fixed (attached to wall)—*Indoor only.*
Space requirements: Length 21 feet, width 9 feet, height 11 feet.

FIGURE B11

Storage: Folds into wall—12" x 11 feet.
Price: American $3000.00 (approx.)
Price: Canadian $2700.00 (approx.)
Distributor:
    Canada:

                Jaffery's Athletic Equipment,
                165 West 6th Avenue,
                Vancouver,
                British Columbia, Canada

Basic Features
1. Permits flexible design.
2. Must be attached to wall—stores against wall.
3. Combination of wood and steel.

Keele Equipment (indoor-outdoor)
Type: Fixed (attached to ceiling).
Space requirements: Adaptable. Minimum size: length 21 feet x width 14 feet x height to maximum of 19 feet.
Storage requirements: Uprights stored against wall, remainder on portable storage rack 6 feet x 3 feet.
Price: Canada: Minimum set $2400.00 to $2600.00, depending upon number of pieces.
Distributor:
    Canada: Jaffery's Athletic Equipment, 165 West 6th Avenue, Vancouver,
             British Columbia, Canada   (2) Raymon & Co., Montreal

    England:
        (3) Keeles of Hadleigh, Ltd.,
        Lady Lane Industrial Estate,
        Hadleigh, Ipswich, Suffolk,
        England

FIGURE B12

Swedish Gym Circuit Training Obstacle Course (outdoor)
Type: Fixed.
Space requirements: Length 22'6", width 12'6", height 7 feet.
Storage: Fixed apparatus.
Price: American $457.00
Distributors: The Delmer-Harris Co.,
                Box 288, Concordia, Kansas, U. S. A.

FIGURE B13

Basic Features
1. Welded structural steel tubing.
2. Easy to assemble (16 sections).
3. Requires concrete foundations.

Lind Climber (indoor)
Type: Portable.
Space requirements: Length 15
    feet, width 4'3", height 4'2"
Storage:

Price: American: $290.00 to $357.00
Distributor: Lind Climber Co.,
                807 Reba Place, Evanston,
                Illinois, U. S. A.

Basic Features
1. Wooden or steel horses available.
2. Adjustable heights for balance beams.

FIGURE B14

Whittle Primary P. E. Equipment (indoor-outdoor)

Type: Portable and fixed.

Space: 5 feet x 15 feet.

Storage: Folds flat.

Price: American: $250.80

Canadian: $287.00

Distributor:

Canada: Fox Gymnasium and Sports Equipment, Amherst, Nova Scotia

England: R. H. Whittle, Ltd., P. V. Works, Montor, Eccles, Manchester

Basic Features

1. Tubular steel.
2. Flexible layout of equipment.
3. Can be erected and dismantled by children.

FIGURE B15

Nissen No. 233 Wall Gym

Type: Fixed.

Space requirements:

12 feet x 9 feet.

Storage: Fixed apparatus.

Distributor:

Nissen Corporation,

930 27th Avenue S. W.,

Cedar Rapids, Iowa, 52406

Basic Features

1. Tubular steel.
2. Folds into wall for storage.
3. Adjustable design.

FIGURE B16

APPENDIX C

Definition of Terms
Used in Movement Education

The following terms will appear in many publications which are concerned with Movement Education. More extensive definitions of each term may be found within this text (see index) or within the references listed at the end of each chapter.

Agility Apparatus: refers to all types of indoor and outdoor climbing apparatus.

Apparatus Work: the third part of a movement education lesson and is concerned with the application of movement ideas to large and small apparatus.

asymmetry: a position or movement which is characterized by unevenness of one part of the body to its opposite side. Using a line drawn through the vertebral column, all positions of twisting, curling or held position, where greater stress is given to the limbs on one side, would be asymmetrical positions.

balance: the ability to hold the body in a fixed position.

body awareness: the way in which the body or parts of it can move (stretch, bend, twist, and turn)

continuity: a situation where movements follow each other in succession.

direct method: in this method of instruction, the teacher structures the classroom organization, chooses the type of activity, and prescribes what each child should perform.

flight: the ability to propel the body into the air.

flow: the ability to link one movement to another with control and efficiency.

general space: the physical area within which a movement takes place.

indirect method: in this method of instruction, the children are given the opportunity to choose the activity or movement idea to be practiced. Class organization and teacher involvement are unstructured.

introductory activity: the first part of a movement education lesson concerned with general warm-up, and lasting approximately five minutes.

level: the relative position of the body or any of its parts to the floor or apparatus. Level may be applied to either stationary activity or position.

limitation method: in this method of instruction, the choice of activity or movement is limited in some way by the teacher.

movement idea: a mental image of an individual movement or a series of movements related to one or more of the basic elements of qualities, body awareness, or space.

movement task: a specific movement challenge created by the teacher or student and performed individually, with partners, in group or on or off apparatus.

movement training: the second part of a movement education lesson and is concerned with the development of movement patterns or sequences on the floor.

pattern: the arrangement of a series of movements in relation to shape, level, and pathway.

personal space: the area around an individual which can be used while keeping one part of the body in a fixed position on the floor or apparatus.

qualities: refers to how the body can move. It is the ability to move quickly or slowly, to perform light or heavy movements, and the ability to link one movement to another.

safety training: refers to the ability of children to move and land in a safe and efficient manner. In the broader context, it refers to the individual's safety on or around apparatus and his concern for the safety of other participants.

sequence: a series of movements performed in succession.

shape: the image presented by the position of the body when traveling or stationary.

space: the area within which a movement takes place.

stretch: moving the body or parts of it from a flexed to an extended position.

symmetry: in movement education, symmetry is used to describe a movement or balanced position where both sides of the body would look identical if an imaginary line were drawn through the middle of the body.

theme: a central movement idea.

time: the speed with which a movement takes place (quick, slow, sudden, or sustained).

traveling: moving in various directions by transferring the weight from one part of the body to another.

turn: rotation of the body and loss of the initial fixed point of contact (e.g., turning in a full arch).

twist: when one part of the body is held in a fixed position on the floor
    or apparatus and the rest of the body is turned away from the fixed
    position (e.g., twisting trunk to the side and back).

weight: the degree of muscle tension involved in the production of a move-
    ment, or the maintenance of a static position involving tension.

APPENDIX *D*

Apparatus, Equipment, and Supply Companies

The accompanying list of companies is listed on the basis of manufacturing and/or selling agility apparatus (indoor and outdoor), equipment (large tumbling mats, springboard, etc.), and supplies (hoops, beanbags, etc.):

American Athletic Equipment Co.,
Box III,
Jefferson, Iowa 50129   —Equipment

American Gym Company, Inc.,
Box 131,
Monroeville, Pennsylvania 15146   —Equipment and Agility Apparatus

Atlas Athletic Equipment Co.
2339 Hampton,
St. Louis, Missouri 63139   —Equipment

Canadian Penitentiary Service,
Mr. J. A. McLaughlin,
Director of Industries for Commissioner,
Ottowa 4, Canada   —Agility Apparatus

Educational Consultants Service,
1393 Greenbriar Way
North Vancouver, B. C.
Canada   —Agility Apparatus

Game-Time, Inc.,
Litchfield,
Michigan   —Agility Apparatus

Gym Master Co.,
3200 So. Zuni,
Englewood,
Colorado 80110   —Equipment

Gymnastic Supply Co.,
247 West Sixth Street,
San Pedro,
California 90733   —Equipment and Supplies
The Delmer F. Harris Co.,
P.O. Box 288, Dept. J.,
Concordia,
Kansas 66901   —Agility Apparatus
Jaffary's Athletic Equipment,
165 West 6th Avenue,
Vancouver,
British Columbia, Canada   —Equipment, Agility Apparatus,
                                           Supplies

Lind Climber Company,
807 Reba Place,
Evanston,
Illinois 60202   —Agility Apparatus
Madsen Gymnastic Equipment, Ltd.,
Unionville,
Ontario   —Agility Apparatus
The Mexico-Forge Climbers,
R. D. 1, Reedsville,
Pennsylvania   —Outdoor Apparatus
Murray Anderson—Olympic Gymnastic
    Equipment,
128 Dunedin Street,
Orillia,
Ontario   —Agility Apparatus
National Sports Company,
360 North Marquette Street,
Fond du Lac,
Wisconsin 54935   —Equipment
Nissen Corporation,
930 27th Avenue, S. W.,
Cedar Rapids,
Iowa 52406   —Equipment and Agility Apparatus
Porter Athletic Equipment,
Porter-Leavitt Co., MFGR,
9555, Irving Park Road,
Schiller Park,
Illinois 60176   —Equipment
A. G. Spalding & Bros. Inc.,
Chicopee,
Massachusetts 01014   —Equipment and Supplies

W. J. Voit Rubber Corporation,
Subsidiary of American Machine and
    Foundry Co. New York,
3801 South Harbor Boulevard,
Santa Ana,
California 92704   —Equipment and Supplies
R. W. Whittle, Ltd.,
P. V. Works,
Monton, Eccles,
Manchester, England   —Agility Apparatus

INDEX

A
Accidents, incidence of, 8
Agility apparatus, 237
Apparatus, 221
Apparatus work, 28
Asymmetry, 237

B
Balance bench, 229
Backward diagonal roll, 142
Body awareness, 14, 155, 237
Bridge shape, 160

C
Cave — Southhampton, 233
Continuity, 237

D
Direction, 176
Direction movements, 93

E
Equipment, 221

F
Flight, 237
Flow, 130, 237

G
General space, 15, 237

H
Human resources, 214

I
Individualized instruction, 11
Individual mats, 222
Introductory activity, 238

J
J.E.G. Equipment, 232

L
Large apparatus, 228
Lesson plan, 25
Levels, 110, 238

M
Methods of instruction, 21
  direct method, 22, 237
  indirect method, 23, 237
  limitation method, 24, 238
Movement Education, 4
  aims of, 5
  definitions of, 4, 21
  structure of, 14
  terms used, 237
Movement idea, 238
Movement task, 238
Movement training, 27, 238

O
Observation of movement, 136

P
Pattern, 238
Personal space, 15, 238
Physical education, 4

Q
Qualities, 15, 118, 238

R
Range of movement, 66

S

Safety training, 33, 238
Sawhorse, 232
Section on places, 43
Sequences, 238
Shape, 238
Sideways tuck roll, 148
Skill progression, 29
Small apparatus, 221
Space, 14, 93, 238
Stretch, 238
Stretching and curling, 167
Symmetry, 238

T

Tails, 105
Themes, definition of, 17, 238
Time, 238
Traveling, 238
Turn, 238
Twisting, 186, 239

V

Vaulting box, 230
Visual aids, 207

W

Weight, 239